A Castle for a Princess

A CASTLE FOR A PRINCESS

POEMS AND SHORT STORIES FOR NICOLE CASEY

JOHNNY WONG

iUniverse LLC
Bloomington

A CASTLE FOR A PRINCESS
POEMS AND SHORT STORIES FOR NICOLE CASEY

iUniverse books may be ordered through booksellers or by contacting:

iUniverse LLC
1663 Liberty Drive
Bloomington, IN 47403
www.iuniverse.com
1-800-Authors (1-800-288-4677)

Because of the dynamic nature of the Internet, any web addresses or
links contained in this book may have changed since publication and
may no longer be valid. The views expressed in this work are solely those
of the author and do not necessarily reflect the views of the publisher,
and the publisher hereby disclaims any responsibility for them.

Any people depicted in stock imagery provided by Thinkstock are models,
and such images are being used for illustrative purposes only.
Certain stock imagery © Thinkstock.

ISBN: 978-1-4917-1285-6 (sc)
ISBN: 978-1-4917-1286-3 (e)

Printed in the United States of America.

iUniverse rev. date: 06/03/2014

CONTENTS

A PLACE OF THEIR OWN

In a place where ethnic minorities still dominated in most major cities across America, right at the heart of New York City, in Belle Harbor the Irish communities still proudly holds on to their culture and history of their ancestry.

As summer arrived, changing colors of leafs plus the growing of grass symbolized the birth of Ireland. Every summer kids, parents, adults and elderly flooded to the beach, first plunged into water every boy dream of becoming Michael Phelps. Every girl loves to swim like Esther Williams.

As evening approached there's magic in the air. They put on a show by the barn fire at the beach. Irish folk songs and dances light up the sky.

When autumn appeared leafs transformed to orange red, sun set arrived early, Belle Harbor reached it forbidden noon.

Little children are dressed up in their beautiful costumes ready for Trick O' Treat. At 8 o' clock huddle of people packed the Q 53 bus ready for work.

When winter came, brought the Casey and Wong family together, the warm spirit of Thanksgiving Christmas signified a time of giving and receiving.

Snow filled the street resembled Bing Crosby, a chorus of a "White Christmas." We watch the building of snow man, with pretty decoration of color full neon light, transforming its neighborhood into a lovely scene.

Being around this ethnic enclave, pride still matter. My nieces and nephew have never forgotten their Irish heritage. In the heart of Belle Harbor, New York, they could proudly proclaimed, a place of their own.

By Johnny Wong

A BABY NAME KELLY

Hi, I am an unborn baby living in my mother belly. Right now, don't have a name yet. I don't know when I will I come out from my mommy womb. Event though I am still inside of her stomach, communicate by kicking, moving, with two little feet.

I ask my parent when will I be born. I keep a diary in my heart. Today the doctor gave me some good news, be born any moment from now.

My parents haven't given me a name yet; wish to be called Stephanie, Stacey, or Kelly. Some day when I grow up I desire to be a doctor similar to my dad, maybe a nurse like my mom. Some say I resemble my father.

My daddy given a name, from now on I will be called Kelly. I feel certain excitement within me. I can't wait to be born, so play with brother and sister.

Kelly you have a four year old sister, Nicky, a brother, Sean. You're precious sister is an adorable person. I think you are going to admire her. Sean first importance is food. This is where he does best in.

Suddenly you appeared on New Year Eve, finally came into the family picture. Obtain the eye of your daddy and have the face of your mommy. We will keep from all harms.

She talks to us by looking at her parents and relatives, by smiling at those who are around her. She wishes to be a ballet dancer, as she's gets older. This is a baby sent from Heaven.

A BANKER STORY

Bright, full of intellect launched her path.

A young college grad. full of confidence ready for a challenge.

Her almamater NYU.

Her graduation ceremony was cum-laude.

First interview energetic.

Every question was magnetic respond.

Interviewer asked "why should I hire you?"

"If you give me a minute worth of your
time, I will make it happen."

Journey of a banker story began.

A journey was striving for glory.

Monies make the world go round and round.

In everybody dream world, a buck speaks louder than words.

Her hard work and determination enable her
co-workers to follow her footstep.

For those who couldn't compete, took sidestep.

Her achievement raised J.P. Morgan Chase to an encomium.

Climbing the economic ladder was like, beating the drum slowly.

Today she's is vice-president of J.P. Morgan Chase.

Full of grace may her story reach to her children's.

By Johnny Wong

A BUCK FOR A LAUGHTER

Rise and shined 6:30 a.m. at higher ground café.

Seeing your humor smiled brighter my day.

The cute funny Texas girl adored my accent.

Your funny smiled tells of Jesus flower plant.

A cup of coffee from a New Yorker jive.

Reflection of your face symbolized Jesus chive.

A smiled, a laughter imparted Jesus character.

If you missed your train at I hop considered to be a laughter.

Every time you sneered at my speech, tells Jesus humor.

God will reserved a flight for a voyage.

All you giggled shined on Jesus brightness.

As I returned home dazzled by your cheerfulness.

Adorable Texas girl could be as funny as Kelly Casey.

Women who loved to giggle happen to be Irish.

Rise and Shined, a buck for a laughter for a Texas woman, who adored the Chinese New Yorker Boston accent. Three cheered for I hoper and their sense of humor.

A CASTLE FOR A PRINCESS

Every girl lived their dream.

In every girl dreamed of their moment.

If she dreamed being fulfilled she's her cream.

Nicole, Carol, if there's an heiress at your request?

Someday, Nicole crowned as your royal heiress, meet her quest.

I could not offer you worldly riches.

If you give me a moment in time a princess will be crowned.

As a child remember packing your goodies.

At sundown your dresses became sprinkling grown.

Knight over pawn to defend your honor.

Castle over rook to safe guard your door.

Queen over bishop defending her majesty.

Pawn over pawn guarding your amnesty.

Knight over pawn, bishop over rook, Queen over
rook, Queen defend King, Queen checked king.

If there is a girl as lovely, as beautiful, as Nicole
for today her handsome Knight dressed in golden
emerald, shining armor ready to kiss Nicki.

For today a castle for a princess.

By Uncle Johnny

A CHAMPION FOR CHRIST

For those who don't know, at the age of
six I was a missionary son.

Born in an unknown land, in an unknown
countries, in an unknown people.

A simple story of my dad, a missionary
pilot, left the comfort of America.

His desired to win lost soul for Christ.

He was a Champion for Christ.

He never won an Oscar, a Grammy award, never
participated in a ticket day parade, yet preaching the

Gospel was his greatest joy.

Didn't knew when his next meal, didn't knew where
his next financial support would be here or not.

Jesus told him "seek first the Kingdom of God
and all these things shall be added to you.

One day, my mom told me the sad news, "daddy is not
coming home, you see Steve, God loves him so much

is time for him to be in paradise.

As I returned to the Amazon, I glanced up toward
heaven, there my dad Nat Saint and Jesus said to him

"well done, good faithful servant, you had won the race,
you had fought the good fight, I'll give you a crown

Of life."

This is the story of his dad, Nat Saint, a Champion for Christ.

By Johnny Wong

A COAL MINER'S SON

At the age of 6 I was a coal miner's son.

I was born on a coal miner story.

Dirt mines, flit mine, copper mine.

Wishing it could be gold mine.

Unfortunately John and Jerry dad was
not born with a sliver spoon.

Deteriorated, their boys were not without hope.

Day and night they proudly waited to see dad arrival.

Coming home from the coal mine he sang the blue.

His dad did not want his boys to follow his shadow.

Someday, somewhere in times knew his sons struck oil.

A day rhyme when they hit the big bucks.

He brought a song from the coal mine.

Days were not short, every precious moment were cherish.

As I imaged boarding the train to the cold mine,
their to greet me was my dad a man full

Of wisdom. BY Johnny Wong

Lyrics taken from Tom Jones "Green Green Glass of Home."

A CUP OF TEA FOR THE FILTHY BRIT

Noon time, tea time, break time, the filthy Brit from Britain,

Cannot start the day without that cup of tea.

Before stepping into my apartment "Johnny do you have tea?"

A China man should know better England stole from China.

China man and Englishman drives on common virtue.

Our friendship grew to be true.

China man and Englishman rely on tea or less no conversation.

Conversation sparks perfection with that cup of tea.

Tea time in Hong Kong and in England our best time of the day.

By three o'clock pleasure and relaxation the best hour of the day.

Monies don't grow on tree, but true friendship fall like leaves.

England and China derive from original roots.

That joint companionship between Johnny
Wong and the Tom Brown School Day

Is nothing but that crazy cup of tea?

The Filthy Brit said to the Yanks "the hell with your coffee."

Without tea you cannot blossom in the state of Missouri.

The Filthy Brit and China man might be
miles apart from each other.

We held photographic memories in our mind.

If your mind can match a dollar "should we have?

That cup of tea old chap."

By Johnny Wong

A DIARY FOR ELISSA

Written in her name.

In a world full of pain.

Comes a day of endless joy.

Words paint a picture.

Image flowed with imaginary.

Words rhymes in poetic.

A diary worth your mind.

Someday you will smile.

My diary a treasure of gold.

First page memories of yesterday.

A story written for today.

Her statement seek not fame or wealth.

Writing built on passion.

Creativity flashed in compassion.

Feeling express in sunshine.

A diary fulfill itself in time.

In his wildest dream come imagination.

Lyric echoed in perfection.

How can a diary fall for you.

Written for your generation.

Elssia might never me offer material
success, gave me the greatest gift.

On this day a diary written for Elissa.

By Johnny Wong.

A DIARY FOR ELISSA

It is written in her name.

In a world so full of pain.

Comes a day of endless joy.

Images flowing in a dream.

Where nothing is as it seems.

A diary worth your life.

Of days without any strife.

Her diary worthy of Gold.

From her days both young and old.

Memories of yesterday.

A story written today.

Creative in compassion.

Her writing built of passion.

Feelings expressed like sunshine.

A diary of all time.

In her wildest dream come imagination.

Lyric echoed in perfection.

How can a diary fall for you.

Written for your generation.

Elssia might never offer me material
success, gave me the greatest gift.

On this day a diary written for Elissa.

By Johnny Wong, revise by IRA Aaronson.

A DIARY FOR ELISSA

A diary written for Elissa.

Words cannot express her kindness.

A picture tells a story.

A diary holds a thousand meaning.

One day she said keep a journal.

Someday you will be surprise.

The day she open my diary.

Words, imaged flowed like heaven.

A generation born in time.

Imaginary, poetic his wondrous dream.

Creation and lyric his wildest fantasy

Details, fantasy rhyme in harmony.

A flash in time sing a story.

I fell in love in writing.

I write until no more ink left.

Melody with joy created in manuscript.

She not afraid to comfort other.

Build her life around Christ.

As we grew older her loves shines brighter.

She had given me so much.

Your birthday heaven brings endless joy.

By Johnny Wong

A GENERATION BEFORE YOUR TIME

People gather by my side. Love to tell a story, a generation before your time. We are all born with gifts and talents. Give me a pen and piece of paper, write a tale that will make you laugh, smile and dance to the beat of Bryan Adams.

When life seems harsh, write you a song about yesterday, tomorrow and today. For we are holy, we are precious. Each day is a struggle, each day problems looks unending. When we wake up, a new beginning, some are bankers, lawyers, teachers, authors, musicians, entertainers and athletics they say good morning to you, black bird singing at the crack of dawn.

For nobody knows what tomorrow bring. If get by today, tomorrow, a new horizontal waiting for us. If I can write in honor of each individual, they can smile, laugh, dance, being a joker that what life is all about.

Sincerely,

Johnny Wong

Lyrics taken from Elton John "Spanish Harlem."

●

A Letter to Madelyn

Dear Madelyn Brittany Wong. You were a precious little darling, 15 months old. You are learning to speak right now, yet not able to. Your "Uncle Johnny" would like to write a letter to you.

The day your mother brought you home from the hospital, if you measured in times, it seem like it only happened yesterday. You must be very tired that day. We whispered to your ear and quickly fell asleep. Go to sleep Madelyn, my dear, rest gently, peacefully and I'll sing you a lullaby.

When your tiny eyes are tightly shut, will fall asleep, begin to dream. You will dream about yesterday, today, and tomorrow. It would turn to many wonderful things, turned into reality. While you're resting peacefully, mommy, daddy, brothers, uncles, aunts, cousins all anxious to meet you, some of the things, happen our beloved country enjoyed prosperity which it had never been before. Uncle Jerry became a stand up comedian, loved to tell his crazy Irish jokes which was very boring, because he needed a bag of new jokes. When Aunt Cindy and Frances saw you, they put their arm around you, like a bear hug. Auntie Margaret baked all kind of goodies, cookies and cheese cake in honor of your name.

Your wonderful brother Eric and Keefe while some refer them as the two little rascals had graduated from their children world. In other news "Uncle Johnny" picked up his old rusted guitar and played until his hand bleed. His writing and lyrics echoed to the sound of a new generation.

Then suddenly your entire dream faded away, you woke up and communicated to us. It would be the dawn of a new day. A new world full of excitements, energies, wonders, acceleration to be meeting, parent held the key which would unlock the future. On this new day mommy as pretty as a Chinese princess, daddy would be a mighty entrepreneur. Your babysitter Karen played with you from dawn to night. She teaches you to smile, laugh and talk. Grand moms change your dapper and nurse you all day long. The Casey Clan had waited long enough to meet you. Lovely Kelly put on a free show. When maturing older, Sean taught you how to play computer, enjoyed watching T.V. When you stood on your toe, Nicole demonstrated to dance to the tune of Swan Lake, first step of ballet.

This is the story of my beloved niece Madelyn Brittany Wong, right now she's only a baby as she grew older, would be happy to read this poem to her audience.

A Lyric for Ben

Words, flowing, drifting upon an ocean wave.

Lyrics flowing end Lessing in his brain.

Melody and harmony rhymed in sweet accord.

If that's a boy, as gifted in music.

On this day talent created in mystic.

Beethoven, Mozart, Schubert his lullaby.

Wealth and fortune not his alibi.

A piano full of his adventure.

His loved for music irreplaceable.

His playing finger spoken verbal.

His playing tells a story of heart being healed.

If there is joy, let our heart be melted.

An anthem, a symphony in his delight.

For his lyrics being crowned as a knight.

By Johnny Wong

A Lyric written for Nicky

Dear Nicky saga derived on every key note of the piano.

Together A, B, C, notes Anglo Casey born on December 1991.

Every good boy fall for Nicole folly.

Good boy admired Nicole dolly.

E note, school in elementary.

A note, advanced in junior high with honorary.

G note gracious Sean Casey your brother.

F note, Kelly foretold your sister.

Treble Clef Casey desired eagerness, fulfilled to gratitude.

G major gorgeous, beautiful, Nicole equaled for fine attitude.

As you strummed G note, graduation from St. Francis De Salle.

Hitting F note, freshman entering Dominic
Academy life lead to melodic.

Admission to Fordham University transformed to harmonic.

If there is a girl as sweet, kind, loving as Nicole A note
rhymed in harmonic with C note equaled B note in

Harmonic style = the song she bring on the
keyboard the tale of an Anglo-Chinese-Girl.

A PASTOR'S LOVE

Life is a wonder, full of heart break, endless struggle.

A compassionate stranger whispered words of humble.

Patient kindness, love, joy, he cherish.

If I could inherited his qualities my best wish.

Dennis dictionary is love multiplied by joy conquer hate.

Goodness divided by cheerfulness equal dinner on a date.

He's soft spoken man of wisdom,

sermon just as mightily as awesome.

Man full of humbleness, gentleness, unique in nature.

His personalities paid wave for t he future.

His heart is of God, greatest asset human desire.

He installed a song sweetly sung by a choir.

As he loves, soft human extended comfort.

Someday our ship in heaven bounded for port.

No words in American dictionary can describe his savior love.

His words can fly peacefully as a dove.

Out of the entire pastor, he is the greatest.

He lived the example of Christ like attitude.

There will be no other wonder pastor in my life to bear his name.

Sincerely,

Johnny Wong

A POEM FOR JULIE MAGORIE

A moment in time with Julie is a moment to cherish.

Our session is so wonderful hate to see it varnish.

Her kindness compassion and
understanding is her code of honor.

Looking into her eyes can picture the reflection
of her personalities in a mirror.

Her personalities are cheerful inspiriting and encouraging.

She knew one day Johnny's writing will be as exciting.

She created hope and joy in our world will be a better place.

If ever returned to school my writing will be an ace.

Always told me tomorrow will be the drawn of a new era.

Understanding people struggle is a good hearer.

If I needed to boost, I boost about Julie greatness.

If I needed to comfort others is a sign of meekness.

How could I express how much joy and happiness?

How could I replace all your goodness?

Consulting and comforting others is your love.

Writing expressing others is also my love.

You could never accept material thing.

Hearing you're wondrous words sparked a ring.

Told me the only way to pay back is thank you.

On this day I gave a piece of my heart to Julie.

Thank you Julie Magorie.   Sincerely, Johnny

A PRINCESS IN PARADISE

A new day, a new way, a new mind.

Today when you walked by wind whispered in your name.

Bird sings in your name.

Heaven holds a place for you.

Adorable princess sparkled.

Adorable bridegroom sprinkled.

Today shines like a morning star.

Today loves filled in a jar.

Heavenly joys in your breath.

Heavenly songs lifted your spirit.

Comes December James be your man.

Comes December said your vow.

Let James charms your name to be holy.

For your name sweet as honey.

Wedding day is time in a bottle.

Pictured angels are singing in anthem.

As Wendell presided eyes glitter.

As James exchanged rings eyes wilder.

On this day Anna banana dream turned into reality.

A beautiful princess kisses her handsome groom.

A wedding held in Heaven.

By Johnny Wong

Lyrics taken from a Christian song "A New Mind."

A RIVER APART

I guessed we knew what separated between New York and New Jersey is the mighty Hudson River.

Life regarding the two states seems to be in comparison and also in contrast. New Yorker and New Jersey residences don't admire each other. People from New York blamed New Jersey folks for leaving the city for a better life, at the same time New Jersey citizens accursed them of creating dirt, crime, noises, and pollution.

As one's journeyed across the Hudson, life seems pleasant, surrounded by hills, trees, houses, similar in stepping to a paradise. Whenever my brother takes me to N.J. to baby sit for my niece, is like to going to a difference world.

Somehow felt great leaving busy restless life of N.Y. behind. There's a sense of happiness going over the other side of the Hudson. Arriving at this place often experienced the warm, quietness, stillness of the summer breeze blowing its gentle wind on a cool summer night.

Then tragedy struck our nation on September 11, 2001, two hijacked airline crashed into the World Trade Center, killing thousand of innocent of people. I do not label these act as terrorist, but racist, because these cowardly cold blooded murder, treachery was mainly motivated by race, their objective were to killed as much American as possible.

Those racist did not know, after the terrible ordeal, New Yorkers and New Jersey residences somehow put their differences aside, created a common bondage, and assisted each other, united together as a nation of all people never to let hate, anger, and vengeance, killing settled in America. New Yorkers and New Jerseys will never forget 9/11.

By Johnny Wong

A SONG FOR EVA

If there a song, a lyric, is for Eva greatness.

C, D, F, notes focus on Christ, dwells on her faithfulness.

D note sleep gently and dream a lullaby.

B notes her boldness lead to her alibi.

G major her goodness, brilliant directed to others.

F major is center on Eva funniness characters.

Whole step, half step equaled Eva holiness.

Octave and interval transform to a beautiful heiress.

E, F, everyday arrived at a tone clothes in armor.

Major and minor chord resembled her grace.

Melodic and interval achieved to ace.

C, B, F notes, in every child brain a world of fantasy.

E, F, G notes Eva fictional grilled on dynasty.

If there a song, in every child dream, I loved to
write a song that speak about Eva loving

Kindness.

From

Johnny

A SONG FOR RACHEL

Look into your hand I see a story unfold.

If you're piano playing can sound pure gold.

The day you received the piano, came into this world.

Magic finger poured out set fire go forth.

Striking a note tells a story of your ancestry.

Ebony and Ivory will rhyme in vestry.

Hitting the A note Johnny nieces Anglo-
Irish-Chinese comes alive.

Rachel melody's as beautiful as Nicole Casey.

Similes and metaphor rhyme in prayer.

Performed magic on piano tells Jesus miracle.

Strikes the C notes Kelly Casey laughter.

Music flows in harmony.

Jesus whispers a song in jubilee.

Sound as loud as Dr. Casey voice.

Familiar tune rejoice in the lord always I said rejoice.

Rachel ballads would transform into a beautiful
princess as Jesus descend to be her bride.

Music sinning tells the story of Johnny Wong Irish side.

A ticket for Rachel, a song melted in her heart,
as ebony and ivory emerged in prayer
room, some day all races would worshiped together in heaven.

By

Johnny Wong

A Story about my Uncle

He was a walking giant, with a gigantic heart, full of compassion with a tranquility, beyond human understanding. His loves for my family and the Fong family was liked steam of honey flowing alone its river bank. His generosity extended to those who had very little on this world.

Even though he struck oil and gold, on the other hand, had never forgotten his family root. He not only love individual in words, but demonstrated through his action.

As I am writing this letter, I found it very difficult letting go of him. In some way, this is a farewell message for my Uncle. It will not be an ordinary farewell, instead his love, compassion, generosity, understanding tells us his reward in Heaven will be great.

I had a Uncle, unlike most relatives, a soft less within him, which extended a quality of mercy, I also believed in many occasion, he also extended a quality of love and a quality of generosity for the Fong family and my family.

Rejoiced and Farwell, you're in a better world right now, both the Wong and Fong families will always cherished, hold special memories of you within our hearts.

Sincerely

Johnny Wong

A SYMPHONY FOR ALAN

A symphony written for him.

Imaged conducting from a balcony.

Words lyrics spoken, gently as an orchestra.

If his music could performed as a howitzer.

A piano, a gentleman, as lovely as Beethoven.

If his harmony and rhymed could flew to Eindhoven.

His gift was similar to a little light music as in Mozart.

His loved for melody became an aviator to Earhart.

Handel, Bach, Schubert, his favorite classical somewhere
in times composing considered mythical.

Lennon and McCarty to be his idolatry.

Somewhere in times Rathe saga became monopoly.

He loved music, speak music, songs and lyrics flew as a flute.

Harmonic and melodic, when girls mentioned
him as cute as Jonas Brothers.

On his birthday a piano, a violin, a guitar, a flute, guided
as an eagle installed within Alan Rathe a masterpiece.

By Johnny Wong

A Tree Grows in Belfast
Northern Ireland

My dear Kelly, I have either, gold, sliver, monies or diamonds to offer you. I cannot give you material wealth of this world, but in the bible said "there are many room, I will come provide a place." There are many mansions that could not be purchased by a millionaire.

There's something you could do for me, give me a pen and a piece of paper and I would write a story in honor of your name. I will write about the history, good times, funny times, joy, sorrow, laughter, struggle, bad times, about my family. You give me the time of the day and I will write a story that transformed you into a beautiful princess.

When you were born on this historic day, a nation came into the picture. This country was where your father, grandmother, uncle, aunt, and cousin. It was where your ancestry came from. As my daddy carried me home from the hospital, everybody was either looking at me, talking about me. When I was born not knowing what to say, the only communication I had, looking at all those funny creatures. Some were fat, skinny, short, and tall, some worn glasses some happen to be loud mouth, laughing, and smiling.

A cold winter day, everybody in the Casey household, we had just finish celebrating Christmas, pretty exhausted. At three before the New Year, my sister Cindy was in labor. Before the mighty hand of the clock struck 12, before the church bell rung they were all very enthusiastic. Then the miracle happen the doctor announced "Kelly was born". The Casey Clan and the Wong families acted like a bunch of wild people, similar to waiting to attend a three ring circus.

Drunkard Gerry asked me not to go to the hospital, because of my mental condition. He didn't want me to jeopardize the safety of both families. Hey "Johnny why don't you write about this historic day, or a poem about Kelly Casey?" He said. "I hear you are a good writer." "Get out of here, my writing couldn't even pay my rent, clothing, food on the table." I said. "I wrote nothing but garbage, so what the big deal." "So made the garbage into a story, you could do that." He mentioned.

As I tried sitting down at the empty house, I quickly pulled out a pen from my pocket; begin brainstorming the garbage ideas, making it into a reality. I wonder why all these people are staring at me? What are they talking? Why are they smiling? Why are they laughing? Am I the center of attention? They must be having a good time, because of me.

Suddenly her head became like an automatic robot. She turned her eyes, similar to a camera zoomed into her lens, took a picture of him writing. What on Earth was this four eyes creature writing? What I am writing was your home country Ireland. Kelly your birth symbolized the culture, people, and history of this nation.

When you were born, freedom, hope, peace, love had finally arrived in Northern Ireland.
 Your world being in 1996, Sin Finn, Gerry Adams right wing, supporter of the Irish Republican Army had finally agreed with British Prime Minister Tony Blair for peace.

When glanced into your tiny eyes, I vision the reflection of Irish Green. I also saw a saga unfolding the tragic struggle, agony, pain, anger, hate and sorrow of Irish Catholic to be free from England control.

My dear Kelly goes to sleep. When you are awaken, will see two suns shining brighten. You will observe both sunset and sunrise together. Whenever the sun is radiant, there's life, so there will be abundance for individuals to share on this Earth. You will see two worlds colliding with each other. As mommy and daddy, age older the old world, my generation will transformed into your generation the new world. In Kelly world, there will be no anger, hate, evil, revenge, killing, no sorrow, no famine, no pain, tragedy, no death. No nation dared to pick up a sword against each other. In January of 1996 hope had finally arrived to the Irish Catholic. A tree grows in the city of Belfast, Northern Ireland.

Ideas and words taken from the movie "2010 A Space Odyssey."

A WEDDING IN CANA

On a hot August afternoon, a wedding took
place in Christian Testimony.

These two lovely couple's had about 300
people gather by their side.

Stan was very sneaky, well prepared with a bag of tricks.

He read his note, all centered on Joanne greatness.

Joanne was trying to hold her tears.

In my mind, I truly witnessed an historic day.

The marriage was like a whole bunch of people,
hugging, laughing and smiling in Heaven.

Joanne, Joanne, may Stan be your man.

Indeed he was your handsome bridegroom.

Indeed, you were a beautiful princess sent
froth from Heaven that day.

Stan and Joanne wedding's Jesus first miracle
at Cana where water turned into wine.

Today is a very happy day.

Jesus gave you new wine.

For today, a wedding took place in Cana.

By Johnny

ALAN RATHE MAGIC TOUCH

You were born with magic in your finger.

I was born with magic in my mind.

Piano strumming create lyric.

Finger writing expressed magic.

Lyric poured out from finger.

Creativity flowed forth power.

Lyric rhymed with force.

Magic charmed with course.

Song led to lyric.

Gong flew to excite.

Alan finger flowed in harmony.

Johnny writing stored in memory.

Lyric, imagery lives in harmony play side by
side on the keyboard and notebook.

One day lyric, imagery and magic light a torch in my diary.

Sincerely,

Johnny Wong

ALP NUMERIC BROWNE

Alp Numeric Browne is my name. Mathematics is my game, think of arithmetic problem, called upon me for assistance. Alp Numeric Browne, sit in his mathematics world, making his arithmetic question for everybody. His world surrounded by addition, subtraction, division and multiplication.

Alp Numeric Browne life is full of arithmetic joys added sorrows subtracted, friends multiplied, love undivided. Addition together with multiplication=master Browne holiness. Subtraction and division=master Browne geniuses.

I do not know anything about Algebra, Geometry, and trigonometry. He is our man, can solve every math problem off the face of this Earth. He is a modern day warrior, armor, full of mathematics solution ready to challenge anybody who gets into his way, equip the mind of a nuclear reactor. Physic x chemistry=Master Browne knowledge. Geometry x trigonometry= Master Browne friendship.

He doesn't have any place to go, lives in a dream world. He thinks, writes, dreams and talks about mathematics all the times. Alp Numeric Data Browne love for mathematics will never ease, it will last forever.

Lyrics taken from Beatles "NO Where Man."

ALP NUMERIC BROWNE

Alp Numeric Browne is my name. Mathematics is my game, think of arithmetic problem, called upon me for assistance. Alp Numeric Browne, sit in his mathematics world, making his arithmetic question for everybody. His world surrounded by addition, subtraction, division and multiplication.

Alp Numeric Browne life is full of arithmetic joys added sorrows subtracted, friends multiplied, love undivided. Addition together with multiplication=master Browne holiness. Subtraction and division=master Browne geniuses.

I do not know anything about Algebra, Geometry, and trigonometry. He is our man, can solve every math problem off the face of this Earth. He is a modern day warrior, armor, full of mathematics solution ready to challenge anybody who gets into his way, equip the mind of a nuclear reactor. Physic x chemistry=Master Browne knowledge. Geometry x trigonometry= Master Browne friendship.

He doesn't have any place to go, lives in a dream world. He thinks, writes, dreams and talks about mathematics all the times. Alp Numeric Data Browne love for mathematics will never ease, it will last forever.

Lyrics taken from Beatles "NO Where Man."

AN ARCHITECT DELIGHT

My name is big bad John

Need an architect designed called on me.

Designing is telling how.

Be great if talent could see.

A child mind full of vow.

His universe surrounded by landscape.

His universe included the poor.

Making end meat in architect no escape.

Be imaginary open the door.

At age 11 constructed a building.

He headed to Berkeley to join the rank.

An architect brain is always creating.

Engineers are happy, many thanks.

An architect work is entertaining.

Constructing landscape is his wonder.

.

No comparison, he's the best.

Expression of architect seems finder.

Glad to be John friend.

Take great pride in his achievement.

By Johnny Wong

.

AND NOW DAVID FOON MAN CHU

A friendship goes round and round.

For October is his birthday.

His name has a sound.

For today his was born in Bombay.

Now beware the Nixon's boys.

True friendship, be blessed in many ways.

First day with a woman, became beach boy.

His poetry, literature, holds an author mind.

His greatness is twisting in the wind.

First time I meet him, man of honor.

His universe filled with color.

Struggling in life became my mentor.

Assisting others is his core.

Thinking more of others is a metaphor.

Forgiving others is his pride.

Friends come and go.

His friendship extended a bridge.

Growing up with David was the best year of adulthood.

By Johnny Wong

ANNIVERSARY DAYS OF OUR LIFE

Women are strange creature.

Women appeared in science feature.

Women are from outer space.

They can break your heart.

One special night, bonded in common interest.

First sight of Stephanie pants on fire.

First sight of Keith eyes on fire.

Peppermint cookies for a date.

Chocolate cookies first rate.

First date monster on campus.

First date together was on a school bus.

Wedding day Bryan Adams sings a tune.

For this day was a lot of fun.

Keith is never cheap with a woman.

Being cheap will regret.

Don't have a dime, can't please a lady.

Listen to a chime, called her daddy.

This is the story of their anniversary, for Keith knew how to spend a buck to please Stephanie

By Johnny Wong

ATOM MAN

I am the smallest element of life, have no beginning nor ending, was discovered about a few decades ago. Some refer to me as the Atom Man. I came from a nowhere land, founded in a nowhere place.

There are three structures inside of me. Protons, electrons and neutrons, combined to form an atom. Proton and neutron reside in the nucleus. Protons have positive charge. The neutrons have no charge, while electrons have negative charge.

I obtained energy from collocating with a free neutron that caused the nucleus to be unstable, in which x-ray, gamma ray and alpha ray to be released. This process was labeled nuclear fission.

Other individual admired me, while other hated me. In 1945 scientists transformed me into a deadly arsenal. The Atom Man was created into an atomic bomb. Our nation had no choice, the enemy refused to surrender, the arsenal save lot of lives on both sides.

Electrons, protons, neutrons, energy for peaceful uses, it will served better than any form of energy. If you had any doubt, please ask the Atom Man for service. I will supply you with all the energy in the world.

Lyrics taken from Beatles "No Where Man."

BEATLETS MANIA

Tonight is a very special night for those who love Rock N' Roll. For all those crazy girls, sit tight, hold on to your seat belt. Tonight will be history. Won't forget what you hear. There had been a lot of talk about this group.

Fans greeted them at J.F.K. airport. "Good evening ladies and gentlemen, I am Ed Sullivan." "These four lads are from Liverpool England." "There's been talked about the British invasion." "Since they arrived in America Rock N' Roll has a new meaning to it." "And here they are the Beatles."

You made us screamed and shouted with "I wanted to hold your hand." Girls started to chase you with "A Hard day Night." In "Can't buy me Love", we danced to the beat of a difference drum. "Twist and Shout" girls came begging on your knee. John and Paul is the creator. George played lead and Ringo set the beat. Then in 1965 the movie "Help" became a legend.

The concert at Shea Stadium blasted Beatles fan out of this world. It created a new message about Rock n' Roll. We felt in love with you when you sung "Yesterday." You created tears in our eyes with "Eleanor Rigby." We got lost in "No man land and became No where land."

We became modern day warrior when "Sgt. Pepper" hit the chart." I became hallucinated in "Lucky in the Sky with Diamond" My mind fell asleep and enter into the twilight zone with "A Day in the Life" Ringo taught me if hard times occurred, we can get "a Little help from my friend."

When "Magical mystery Tour" arrived, you created a fantasy world for us to live in. "Strawberry field" desired for me to eat Strawberry ice-cream. "All you Need is love" came out, we all felt in love." When dispute or controversy arrived you told us "We can work it out."

When strangers and friends occurred in our life you taught us to say "Hello Goodbye." As I toured my neighborhood "Penny Lance" rings in my ear. As I listened to the radio, I became know as the "Fool of the Hill." When my prestige disappeared, I became the "Fool of the Hill."

When my lyric became popular, then "My Guitar Gently Weeps," we rebelled against authority when "Revolution" occurred. As the violence and destruction grasp us "Hey Jude" let us know there's a better place to live. Sunshine was always with us in "Here Comes the Sun." You bit us farewell and goodbye in "Let it be."

Rock n' Roll artist come and go, but the Beatles are here to stay. We treasure there song all our life. There memories have a special place in our heart. As we grew older their lyrics became more popular.
When Beatles mania came alive, they were born again.

Lyrics taken from Linda Ronstadt "Difference Drum."

BELFAST 'S CHILD

Kelly my dear I have no wealth or fame.

Nothing I can offer.

Write in honor of your name.

A story seems kinder.

A story transformed to princess.

A story seems tender.

A nation confesses.

A nation seems finer.

Your birth is a historic day.

Ireland came to play.

A nation cried unto you.

A nation wished to be free.

A miracle fore told.

Irish Catholic, pain, anger, struggle enfold.

How can Ireland cried for you.

How many innocent lives are shed?

Birth of Kelly a county was being healed.

She is children of Belfast.

Kelly mourned for children of Belfast.

January 1996 Belfast's child was born.

By Uncle Johnny

BRENDA UNIVERSE

Dear Brenda I could not afforded to purchased you the material thing in this world. In John 14 before Jesus departed from his disciples he said "in my father house there are many mansions, that could not be purchased by a millionaire."

Brenda nobody said the Christian life was easy, not always full of joy, happiness, God doesn't blessed us all the times, but during those difficult circumstances, he searched our heart.

Just imaged heaven is a day away, heaven is so huge, better than this present universe, where in Heaven, there will be a room for each individual. In this present world room is exchange for rent, but in our heavenly father world, it is deliver to us when we departed from planet Earth.

They once mentioned the great Ted Williams was the last man in major league baseball to bat 400, he had vision in which he could view the entire baseball field.

Brenda just imaged Heaven is a place so vast, take all your difficulties' there and God will prepared a place when you leaved Earth.

Brittney Got no Monies
to buy Chinese Food

A buck for an Egg Roll, a buck for a Spring
Roll, a buck for a Chicken Roll.

How long is a China man, how long can
you survive without Chinese Food.

Poor Brittney she did not know Johnny, who's a high roller.

She did not have monies to purchased Chinese Food.

The day she burned her veggie she starved.

If FSM girls were rich, be a shock wave.

FSM girls were bunch of phony.

Yet they were needy.

Do not have Chinese Food cannot
consecrated on Alan Hood lecture.

Imaged cooking international cuisine spiced up a picture.

Since girls don't know how to cook, they were not very mature.

Pork Fried Rice, Shrimp Fried Rice, Chicken
Fried Rice served under your delight.

If FSM girls stomach were full, they rocked the clock tonight.

Soul Food, high five, slapped me five, if Johnny
could cook you girls a Chinese meal.

A friendship round as a ring.

Food goes round and round in heaven.

For I do not know Brittney, if ever returned to I hop, in my dream,
loved to give her six dollars to chow down at the Chinese Buffet.

CARISSA LAUGHTER

When babies are born, they're special.

All babies are given names, before birth.

Her name is special, her name is Carissa.

Beautiful name rhymes with Melissa.

A beautiful name, for an infant.

Every child cried of innocence.

Every laughter, a sound of joy.

Her laughter, a sound of pleasant.

Little girls love to charm.

Children enjoy possessing toy.

Talks Jesus, prays Jesus, loves Jesus.

Meditate dreams on God holiness.

Early age received gift of prophesy.

Gift of prayer are mighty and awesome.

Forgiving others is her answer.

Loving God tops all layers.

For I only spoke with Carissa, twice, her laughter
and forgiveness inspire me, that we

Can work things out, for live is very short.

By Johnny Wong

CHILDRENS OF THE 90'S

Here's to the children of the 90's. We were baby-boomer of the forties and fifties, came out from our mother womb during post World War 11. Our parents took real care of us. We grew up where the country was full of luxuries, lived in a world of conveniences and plentiful, didn't understood what it was to starve or to be in needs. Mom and dad provided for us.

While we were gently sleeping in our cab, some events took place. In 1946 Communists took over Eastern Europe. 1948 Berlin Wall set up by Russia. 1949 Communists win control of China.

Our universe considered special, resided in a generation, apart from our parents. The world was a fantasy, which consisted of famous teen idols such as Elvis Presley, the Beatles, Beach Boys and the Rolling Stone.

A young nation with the economy blooming, begin controlled by the baby-boomer. They wanted to challenge the universe. We grew up in the decade where John F. Kennedy was sword into office. His desired for us was to be the defender of the free world.

We witnessed the Beatles invasion; saw them in the Ed Sullivan show, saw first man to walk on the moon, fought for environmental and women rights, the establishment of the Peace Corps. We danced to the music of Buddy Howdy and Richie Vale. For those days it was great and fun to be labeled as a liberal.

Title taken from Joan Baez song "Children of the 80's.

COMMENCEMET ADDRESS FOR KELLY CASEY

Kelly if you give me a minute in time, a miracle foretold, in honor of your name.

My dearest Kelly, may your days be full of wines, roses, sprinkled flashes by.

For today, a new day, a new wine, let us come gather by her sides for she had graduated

From her childhood world, to day as you wake, dawn of a day, of new era.

 Black Birds singing in the crack of dawn, sky opened shower of blessing overflowed your hair.

As you walked up to pick your diploma, mom, dad, Sean, Nicky, godmother, godfather, aunts, uncles, grand mom, grand father, aunts and uncles are all mighty proud of you.

As you approached the podium, imagined each step embarked the journey of a beautiful princess saga. Your name was special; parents called you Kelly, a very pretty Irish baby.

On Kelly christen, Bell Harbor transformed itself into an adventured, fantasy, wonderland for children to play in.

When she learned to play the keyboard, the mountain shook, oceans spread apart, sun brighten, moon shined, stars fell from Heaven.

When she's auditioned the lyric "Shenandoah", her voice echoed to the tune of new generation. A generation where musicians like Bryan Adams, Phil Collins, the Beatles, Richard Marx, James

Taylor, Air Supply, Journey, and Christopher Cross will always hold special memories.

The day she's received her diploma there was tears and joys in our hearts.

My dear Kelly how could you ever repaid Uncle Johnny, God parents father, mother and the rest of the Wong and Casey clans?

My final answered to her, Kelly someday when you become a famous actress and you got a part in a Broadway Play, that's how you could repaid us.

CONGRATULATION KELLY!!!

By Uncle Johnny
Lyrics taken from Wes Terasaki "A New Wine."

Lyrics taken from a Christian Song "A New Mind, A New Way.

Lyrics taken from Beatles "Black Birds."

COOKIES FROM MAGGIE

Maggie my dear, your cookies as sweet as cherries, whenever I left home for another place mom would tell me, Maggie baked some goodies for you. As I ventured to Urbana Illinois, her oatmeal cookies cheer and wheel my adventured. At the arrival to Boston, chocolate, raisins, coconuts, maple nuts, told me success will brighten the future. As I journey to Toronto Canada, honey, raspberry, blueberry, jelly cookies, assimilated into a true Canadian. When I got a job offer in New Jersey, honey mustard, golden mustard served on an afternoon delight. As I packed my bags for the British Crown Colony of Hong Kong, crackerjack, on top of smoke jack, wishing my flight will never be hijacked.
While I was the Midwest of Kansas City, sugar crumb, honey crumb, raisins crumb, sent a clear message Maggie goodies not far behind.

A cookies as cute, round as a friendship, yet it seems funny happiest moment resembled our wonderful stories the size of a cookies.

COOL HAND DIXON

They called me "Cool Hand Dixon and me purchased a 12 string guitar in a garage sale. We tried to form a band, but it didn't last. David quit, went back to school. Joey fell in love with a girl, varnished in the divine wind.

Contrast to other guitarist, he played with a full force of rhythm and force. He could perform either right handed or left handed. When he touched that instrument, the rhythm flows in his hand. His guitar playing attracted all kind of people.

People on planet Earth let's made a song request, so cool hand Dixon could play for us. During the Presidential inauguration cool hand Dixon performed in front of 12,000 screaming fans. What ever song a person writes cool hand Dixon, does it ten times better than anybody else.

Similar to an author writing a book, cool hand Dixon speaks through us his guitar playing. The way he plays his guitar, he tells a story to us. It is similar to a human.

When it is happy, it sounds loud. When it is sad it sounds slow. In a love theme cool hand picked the strings to get that beautiful sound. Nobody could do it better than cool hand Dixon.

Lyrics taken from Bryan Adams "Summer of 69'."

Dear Daniel sister, I left God wanted me to write this letter to you. Please forgive my spellings and grammars I just too lazy to check it.

I wanted to write something special to you, that is the Sunrise Social Club House, which meet a couple of weeks ago. Let me tell you something each of our members are unique, we are special, we stand out among the average population of a well know nation which is rich in all areas of lives, on the other hand we are among the few that are left out.

We are the forgotten Americans or the one left out from the average success group of Americans. Our beloved nation put sigma on us; some refer to us such as the mentally ill or insane, retarded, sociopath, and ignorance. Our lives are hurt or threaded by all these medical terms which label us.

On this day we gather together as a family to discuss our illness, difficulties and talk about ways which we can assist each other.

Today we struggle to get by our common problems such as getting out of bed, washing up, getting dress and leaving our homes. Most normal people had no trouble in coping these tasks.

We know we are not alone in these struggle, encounting the same issues. We request one favor from our nation, never to forget us, we are not asking for royal treatment, just wish to be treated similar to common folks. Many of us will not hold full time job, creating a sizable income. Will never being on the on the cover of New York Times magazine, winning an Oscar award nor famous authors. Our ear tune deaf, no ticket day parade to honor us.

On the other hand we accomplished one thing normal people over look. With the trickling of the clock we manage through each day. We know our problems never go away, yet we constanting never give up hope. As night and silence arrive over us, we give ourselves some credit, that we live thought that particular day and over come the ordeal. We more or less struggle, that is our only and true victory, to those who are still ill it is considering our greatest victory.

To Daniel please carry this letter wherever you go, when circumstances arise, take it out and read it.

Sincerely,

Johnny Wong

Dear God

I remembered when George Bush was running for president back in 1988; his speech "he wanted America to be a softer, gentle and kinder nation. During that period, I too wished to be a kinder, gentle, compassionated person.

God deep down, I failed you a hundred, maybe even thousand times. For me is mostly talked, often people accursed us Christian as hypocrite, well I hated to say it, I fell into that category.

God, I cannot and do not understand, why someday, I shared the Gospel and one day, when things turned worse, why on Earth I cursed your name.

Similar to what person Bush commented, I wanted to love, understand and be more compassionated person too. I guess it is a challenge for us, to love, forgive, to do good for those who done evil, cruel, said, show, anger toward us.

If I am sharing my faith for my family, siblings, my nieces and nephews, I also must have forgiveness in my heart on these White women's, Black men, Chinese people, plus some Caucasians bosses who haven't treated me with respect.

Dear Jesus Christ, I cannot promised you anything, with your strength, grace, I know the Christian life is never easy, if I failed big times, please forgive me. When people had wrong me, disappointed me, I don't know how to love these people, let me gain my pride, by simply walking away to avoid any confrontation.

Dear Jesus, I am very thankful that you provided Eva for consulting me. She's very understanding, compassionated and helpful. I often looked for forward in meeting with her. I recalled during those times with Elissa-Lin-Rathe, she's very eager to see my writing, the same holds true for Eva.

Diary of an American solider in Normandy

Dear Mary heart of gold, lips as sweet as cheery. Face full of pink daisy. Smiled radiated liked sunflower. Today was June 6, 1944, I am writing this diary to you on a landing craft bounded for the invasion of Normandy France. Our supreme Allied commanders, Anglo-Americans label this day as D-Day, meaning "Dooms Day."

Eisenhower, gave us a prep rally announcing this to be our greatest day in history, because we were going to returned France to liberate its people from Nazi occupied Germany. Their leaders, their nations, people waiting years to be free. He warned us some or most of us will not returned, most likely be killed by enemies fired. He desired each of us to do there utmost duties, services for the Americans people back home. He stated "our job, considered to be very vital in defeating Hitler Nazi Germany in brining to the war to the end." "Even though most of you will be perished before you hit the beach of Normandy, on the other hand go and give them hell." He said. "Today our beloved country United States people back are mighty proud of you."

Dear Mary our target co-named Omaha Beach. In the background, I could hear the mighty thundering of 16, 14 inch. Gun of our battleship, its shell roaring on the beaches of Normandy. As I viewed the sky the flares of rockets, liked Fourth of July fire work racing toward the sandy beaches. As I turned my eyes to the left, I saw Dauntless Dive Bomber, p-51 Mustang, and p-47 Thunderbolt fighter armed with bombs ready to unleashed on the enemies artilleries.

Dear Mary we're about half way to the beaches. I am very nervous and scared. What happened if I don't made to the beach? What happened if our mortal shells or artilleries shell landed on our landing craft killing all of us? What happened if I get shot by a sniper?

"O.K. men this is it, let's moved it out." Shouted the lieutenant. "Mary I am going to put this diary away in my body, for now on, going to communicated through my mind."

Once the landing craft dropped their door, I witness men around me helplessly, rapidly falling face down to meet their terrible ordeal, Eisenhower was absolutely correct many of us were killed by German machines guns bullets and mortal, artilleries shells. They were killing us similar as practicing as shooting galley. I could see arms bodies flying all over the places. Bloods spreading on the beaches, friends, buddies crying out in agonies. Mary this is no dramas or faction, this is not a movie, this is war and in real combat, men killing each other.

Mary please asked God to spare my life, if he could get me out of this mess, I promised I won't gambled, won't have sex, won't smoked, no longer get into physical or verbal confrontation with any bodies. I will never tasted the smell of alcohol beverages'. I will still wished to marry you and be the best handstand in life.

By two to three hours, everything was over, the whole ordeal finished. We finally secured the beach head. Unfortunately casuistries were very high over 2,000 men killed or wounded. It took us a couple of more hours to bury our dead comrades.

By night fall, as tried as we happened to be, we slowly inch step by step to reach the city of Paris. At dawn one could hear the sound of birds if they were sinning. We all felt the chill of the morning frost. Light rain gently fell among us. The strong smell of our odor, let us know when is time for a shower. Within the next hours sunlight radiated, symbolized there's hope for each men, made a shiny path for us to guide us to victory.

Later on we dug fox hole in wait for the enemies to arrived. I decided to take my diary, once again wrote to Mary. "Dear Mary thank God I had made it this far." "I have a good feeling I am going to survive this terrible war." "I had seen men dieing, many of them crying in pain." "On the other hand our morale is very high." "We all loved to go to see that beautiful city called Paris." "The French civilians was very kind, nice and generous to us, they offered shelter and foods for many of us." "Without their assistance, it might be very hard to get by." "Have you get a chance to say hi to my parents, brothers and sisters?" "Are you going to have a delicious supper tonight?" "The French Farmers feeds us quite well, they gave us chickens, cheese, steaks, French bread and pasties with milk to drinks." "I am sorry Mary once again, I must put away my diary, needed to prepared to wait upon the enemies."

Then suddenly without any warning a mortal shell landed on top of his foxhole, one fellow soldiers saw him groaning in pain. He shouted "medic come here, we have a wounded solider in pain." He started to whisper to himself my God, what hit me, why is this happening, what exactly when wrong? "Don't worry Private, let me check you out, I'll tried my best to save you. "Don't brother I don't think anybody could save me, not even you." The solider responded. "I know who can save you that's God and Jesus Christ." "I been a good person in life and I go to mass and confession almost every Wednesday and Sunday." "Private we're not going to Heaven, because of our good work, instead we're going to Heaven by what Christ did for us on the cross and repented of our sins." "Do you want to ask Christ to come to your heart?" "Yes I do." "My diary in my back pocket, please made sure it gets to my girl friend back home Mary." "Yes I made sure it will." Then the soldier closed his eyes and passed away. The medic took his hand and said "thank God you're in peace and in heaven right now, please rest in peace.

ELISSA COMPASSION

If there is a moment in time, would write about a pretty, lovely, kind, gentle, compassionate, woman ever to embark on planet Earth.

She's doesn't do anything fancies or speculated, yet those words continued to ring in my ear, "Johnny to this day, please keep a diary."

I don't deserved any credits, if it was, coming through God from her. She quoted "a picture is worth a thousand words." "A diary is worth a thousand meaning, it paints a thousand images, stored millions, hundreds of memories."

Elisa mentioned "writing is not so much in accumulation of wealth and fame; one must desired a passion for writing."

Elisa someday when I am not around "how will you wanted to remember me?" I wished to be recognize as a person who could write to individual, who are suffering either physically, or mentally, if there was a smiled on their face, even if they could never verbalized, thank me in person that's how I choose to remember.

Sincerely,
Johnny Wong

ELISSA LIN RATHE LOVE DESIRES CONQUERS ALL FEAR

Elissa wondrous compassionated words flowing as poetic.

Johnny to this day please keeps a diary its story will eclectic.

Imaginary, poetic, rhythm, lyric will startled Elissa mind.

My writing will be as sweet as cheerful when you kind.

Shakespeare, Joyce and Hemingway
could never achieve their fame.

Give me a pen it will sparks a fire like flame.

She knew one day my writing lead me to a better person.

If writing could prolong suffering on
Earth must not be postpone.

Elissa knew imaginary excel to perfection.

Combining with poetic life excel in motion.

Story telling, narrative, journalism explore our inner self.

She knew sunshine will brighter as an elf.

An author world has no beginning or ending.

If writing could scowled like an eagle wing.

Spelling and grammar should never prohibit one's creativity.

Someday my mind flew at speed of sound insured objectivity.

Knew writing opened new chapter in people life.

Words could blow gently as a leaf.

Johnny writing will echoed to beat of a difference drum.

Included rhythm, simile, metaphor add up its sum.

Imaginary, creativity comforted suffering conquered all fear.

Elissa love, joy added kindness, subtracted anger, hate, multiplied, happiness, cheerfulness equal Elissa greatness.

EPIC OF OUR TIME

Children listened to a story in your time.

Give us the time, girls danced and smiled.

Lyricists flowed from Liverpool England.

Fame and fortune, America here we come.

Night to remember, Ed Sullivan Show.

Lennon and McCartney set the stage.

Tell us a story in your name.

Lyrics more precious than Gold or Silver.

Songs set the tune of a nation in turmoil.

Give us a song, if we could change the world.

Someday world never the same.

Write in honor of your name.

How can McCartney fall for you.

How can Lennon sing for you.

Story telling love to boost.

We will write where hate is gone.

Imaginary flowed through fantasy.

Our music rhyme in harmony.

People let us sing a chorus in anthem for Lennon
and McCartney wrote music a generation

Before our time.

The saga of Lennon and McCartney, epic of our time.

By Johnny Wong

Lyrics taken from "One-Tin Solider."

Lyrics taken from "American Pie" Don McLean.

ERIC'S THEME

Earthly runner, runs for glory.

Heavenly runner runs a better race.

Every runner, there's a story.

His name can't be replaced.

His name recorded in history.

Dawn of a new day.

Dawn of a new Olympic.

Runner runs in a race.

He runs rhythmic.

He is the price of Scotland.

His name was Eric Lid dell.

Flying Scotsman reigned in his land.

His racing was foretold.

Running a race, has no formula.

Commit to Christ is the formula.

Jenny "God made me fast."

"I run for his pleasure."

On this day Brother Wendell and Brother King
Sermon, forgetting what behind and straining
toward what is ahead. Let us think of Eric Lid dell
carrying the Gospel to the nation of China.

By Johnny Wong

Lyrics taken from Honey Tree "Maratha Marathon."

Eva Action

You're the greatest when you reached out to me.

You're the boldest when you cared for people.

You the kindest when you took interest on others.

You the smartest when your strategies paid off.

You're the sweetest when nobody seems to care.

You're the bravest, when you took a step forward.

Chorus for Nicole

In another land, in other time, in other places,
my darling Nicole, you're the greatest.

You are more precious than sliver or gold.

From Johnny Wong

EVA COMPASSION

What is a job?

Is it achieved wealth?

If monies are answer, must stop.

Some emphasized on health.

Need a solution, called on Eva.

She will not add complication.

Compassion ear extended.

Her passion extends an arm.

She is not fancy.

She conduct simple task.

She cares as a nanny.

She doesn't think any less of other.

Love she received, she cast on other.

First meeting, she loves people.

Understanding suffering is the answer.

Never condemn, search the finder.

Never in anger, demonstrate positive.

With Eva even achieving one percent

She would spoil you with praises.   BY Johnny Wong

FAREWELL TO TARGET AT HICKSVILLE

I just finished applying for an employment on the terminal for a position at Target Department Store. I picked up the red phone; spoke with the operator "I just completed the application process." "We are conducting interview next week." She said. "When will a good time be for you, to come in?" She asked. "How about Wednesday at 11 a.m.?" will that be o.k.?" "That will perfectly be fine; we will give you a call." She answered. "Thank you very much and have a nice day." I responded.

As for me, never wished to celebrate too early, ever since, leaving college in 1985, had close to about 300 interview, resulting in very little success, mainly rejection, some sounded impressing, promising, but the last minutes was similar to hitting a split finger fast ball.

The split finger fast ball considered the most deadly pitch to swing at. It seems like the perfect ball to bat against, unfortunately the last second, ball dropped from the strike zone, most batters struck out foolishly. At the same circumstances, feeling optimistically, because in the past, when I applied for the Target at Elmhurst at Queens Blvd. about four times, once they guaranteed to interview me, but never delivered.

I had just gotten back from Kansas City, things didn't work out over there, and friend disappointed me. Once again back in New York for the fourth time.

The day of the interview, similar to a general planning out its strategy, opened up a new White Shirt, which purchased recently, put new my favorite red tie and khaki dress pant.

It was mid June, as I stepped out the house, blazing sun, glazing on my shoulder, smell of green grass; remained summer was in the air.

Target happened to be located at North Broadway Mall. Once called Mid-Island plaza in Hicksville New York, the last time, I been to that shopping mall in September of 1983, going out with a girl named Carol.

I got to the bus stop at Flushing Main Street, there were about 25 people waiting in front of me for the N20 bus to Hicksville train station, of all the buses, this one considered the most crowded. We were packed like Sardine in a tin-can.

I sat next to the window on my way to Hicksville, got to observe the scenery of Nassau County. A brief history concerning, Nassau and Orange Counties, probably the highest per capital income of any residential places in the United States.

As the vehicle slowly approached C.W. Post Long Island University, memories of Carol kindled in my heart. I would said she was your average Italian all American girl. New York Yankees, N.Y Islander, Billy Joel, Beatles, what hamburgers, meatballs, hot dogs, blue berry pie to American favorite past time.1

When I first encountered her, she was studying to be an actress, invented me to one of her play, she portrayed to absolute perfection.

"Broadway Mall" the bus driver said. Once I got off, like stepping toward a museum park, could hardly believe 24 years ago remained me of a difference universe. Those days labeled as Mid-Island Plaza, because the town of Hicksville happened to be mid way between Nassau and Suffolk Counties. To my surprise the shopping mall had decreased a little in size. The architectural seems pretty amazing. It composed of many retail business and restaurant.

I walked into the Human Resources office Alice, the receptionist, very pleasant and nice to me. She told me "to have a sit." About half-and hour later, the Human Resources Manager called me into his office, very friendly, nice, down to Earth, introduced himself to me, his was Ronald.

One question seems rattled across his mind. "Johnny how flexible is you?" He asked. "Can you work on weekend, Saturday, Sunday, nights, days or holidays?" He questioned. "Oh I am very flexible, I could worked any time of the day. I told him. "Since you don't reside in Long Island, would it be a major problem for you getting here?" "Definitely not, there's the N20 Hicksville Nassau County transportation, which takes me directly to the mall." "I could also travel on the Long Island Rail Road." "I also take the Long Island Rail Road." He said. "Johnny due to your flexibility, I am going to offer you a position, right now.

"Wow I couldn't believe what I am hearing." "My head felt almost striking the ceiling." I said to myself. He didn't brother to check my employment references. Not only was he nice, but when a manager gave you a position on the very first day, that tells what kind of character he possessed.

After his statement I somehow sensed his employees must have a lot of good things to say in regard to him. He shook my hand, told me to go next door to obtain a drug test and they're called me in for orientation.

Before I left Human Resources Office, somehow, knew we struck a wonderful friendship, in which it would last unit the final days at Target.

Unlike most employees, right away, sensed he wasn't there to collected that fat check, like most people do, understood, deep down inside, he cared, took the time and reach out to his co-workers, whenever they encountered issues.

Next Wednesday arrived for orientation. Ronald assistance gave a speech, a general outlined in regard to store policies, in how to interact with customers. We saw a video on sexual harassment. It demonstrated interaction between men and women, on what to do, or not to do, such as inappropriate contacts or speeches.

That was far from my concern. The main issues happened to be racism against Black people, struggling with these issues for about 21 years, made little process, then fell away, time after time.

Some of the words, kept echoing inside, "no matter what you do, if caught into a verbal, physical confrontations, I had everything to loose, they got nothing to loose." "If you are not ready, don't feel comfortable sitting, standing, staring a Black person, then quietly get up and remove yourself from that situation.

The last time I employed was back in 2004, so been for a while, Target going to be the testing ground. How individuals, Blacks viewed me, made an impacted on "what type of person Johnny Wong is." Is he a cruel, evil, revengeful, type which, would lead to argument or fights with co-workers.

Since the mental illness, suffered for so many years, am hopping everybody, if not, most people would be understandable. It wasn't something, which go away over night. It will take many years, step by step, one day at a time.

I needed to remain myself, Blacks are not perfect, not all going to treat me nicely. They are similar to most people on Earth, not superman, don't have too high of an expectation from them.

They're just ordinary person who had problems like us. I had lost many jobs in the past, because of confrontations with Afro-Americans. Somehow deep in my mind, wasn't going to let history dictate itself.

The following day, reported to work. First big test, in back stock room, the first person to introduce to me, his named Abdul a Black fellow, to my surprise struck a pretty interesting conversation with him.

Later on he introduced Omar an Arab, both of them were willingly to teach me, not only were they helpful, went out of their way to assist me whatever they knew how. Words has a way of expressing itself through them, even if I created about 100 errors in pushing or pulling the items, stocking products on the wrong shelf, they still continued to treat me nicely, never having any angry words at me.

At this particular moment, noticed the job right away, as boring as hell. They told me "to work on the back stock order, meaning to remove items from the cart and placing it on the correct shelf.

Out of the blue, as I was climbing the ladder to place a product on the shelf, a cool duce named Peter Son came up to the ladder, extended his hand to greet me. "Wow, what a start, what a way to go, today is bran new day, for those who are familiar with baseball; I am battling close to 300.

I told him I was very nervous being first day on the job, didn't knew too much about the stock room. I said "I am slow, made huge mistakes similar to being the new kid on the block. "No that quite o.k. you had nothing to be afraid of, I am here with you, work beside me, you're do fine." He said.

He was kind of like the Lone Ranger assisting me, in a crisis, taught me how to point the gun, equipment, we handle at Target, told me to aim at code bar, advising me on how to position myself at certain direction, angle and stood at a certain range of your body. Peter let me knew if firing the gun, meaning pressing the button, will receive a funny sound. If no sound appear, something went wrong. The materials won't process.

Next step demonstrated in showing me, how to pull, taking items off the stock room. I desired to mention, since being a rookie, not used to the challenge, on the other hand, possessed a lot of confident in me. He explained certain number, when punched into the gun, plus, counting how many items were left in the boxes.

There was another fellow, pretty cool duce, his name was Lamont, wasn't very close with him, on the hand, he always looked out for me, telling me, did I take the 45 minutes lunch and 15 minutes breaks.

The next day, I was introduced to the big chief in the back stock room. When I first lay eye on him, knew right away, a great guy. His name was Bob, happened to be your average person, very down to Earth, and never had any harsh words with anybody in Target.

First day working alongside him, felt like superman. "You're doing one hell of job with the back stock Johnny." He said. From what I viewed of this person, difficult it may seem. I doubt if he had any enemy in Target. It was like telling me "Johnny welcome to the back stock room, don't worry, we're take good care of you, today your one of the family."

Fritz was the next cool duce. I was a little afraid; begin new in the stock room, of asking him any question. He looked tough from the ghetto. A little shocked told me "if I had any question, don't be scar of letting him know."

One major thing, we shared in common, both a big Mets fan. I explained "I am born before your time, when the Mets got the best pitching staff, consisted of Tom Sealer, Jon Mat lack, Jerry Kosmas. Conversation got real hot, as we said "they were the best team in wining the World Series back in 1986, against the Boston Red Socks, 4 games to 3.

This is how we described game six at She stadium, the Red Socks, head by one run. Moonie Wilson headed up to bat, the tiding run on third base. Boston one out away in capturing the World Series, count was full, three balls and two strikes, Moonie fouled the last couple of pitches out of place.

Then a mighty strange thing occurred, he hit a slow grounded toward Boston first baseman Bill Bunker. Right away it looked like a routine play. "Moonie had good speed." The announcer said. The last minutes, he took his eyes from the ball, to Moonie, instead of playing it safe, by placing the glove on the ground, the ball took a funny hop, ran through Bunker leg and the tiding run scored the Mets again alive, went on to win game six and were champion.

The next duce that came into the picture, none other than "Big Sean", and nobody messed around with him, he's a big touch duce, and he studied martial art, so nobody dared to get on his case. What's interesting he said "he had some Chinese Blood? probably from Jamaica, quite a few Chinese Jamaican, beside Jews, Indians, and Whites. I assumed the Chinese usually the wealthiest, because almost every one loves Chinese food. I recalled I spoke with a Black fellow while working in Boston in 1989. I said to him "us Chinese don't give anybody a hard time." His immediately response "but you people give us good food."

Lamont told me "to go for lunch around 2 p.m., went to the Food Coop at the mall, very crowded as hell. Everything considered high price, don't need to worry the Chinese restaurant stealing business from other fast food places, didn't matter what kind of individual, they all enjoyed Chinese food.

I had fry rice with vegetables, consisted of some delirious steaks and shrimps. He asked me "what's your name?" I told him "Johnny." Next thing, he noticed my Target Badge, he pointed a sign to me which said "all employee mall gets 10% discount. I mentioned to myself "boy there's a real treat."

As I headed back toward work, meet another funny character, this person happened to "Little Sean," to differential himself from "Big Sean." Little Sean a wild duce, his mouth similar to a fire cracker, for him life assumed to be a joyous big roller coaster ride. Most occasion I hardly sensed he's never in a bad, depressing, angry mood, never saw him firing full ammunitions, meaning giving harsh words to people.

The idiot considered himself as working in a three ring circus. Next he asked me "if I ever been in bed with any women?" When I responded "no" to him," told me I was way behind the game, battling below 300, since never had sex with any women, the count 0-2, stating I had two strike in life. He let me knew, he wanted to set me up, hell I didn't cared if he offered some soul mama, Indians, Latinos, or fair skin women.

To be honest with all you folks at Target, I once worshiped White women like diamond and gold. I spend monies, cooked for them, purchased gifts for this group of girls, never once they said "I was cute or good looking." For over 30 years, these women got the nerve to take, grabbed from me, never gave me anything back in life, so what the hell when these Blacks, Indians, and Latinos said "your cute and handsome," that showed non- White girls very pleasant to hang out with, while White girls happened to be very racist toward us Asian men.

Later on I found it hard to consecrate on my work. An ugly battle field waging in my mind, to those who don't know too anything regarding mental illness, I struggled with O.C.D., stood for Obsessive Compulsory Disorder, a very severe sickness.

There were days, if any one who hurt my feeling, directing or in directing angry words against me, found it extremely difficult in getting through the day, without obsessing over the issues.

Two months ago, gotten back from the International House of Prayer in Kansas City, many of the young kids there, assisted them finically, never brother to get back in touch with me.

In my brain, waging an angry confrontation with this group of people, the only solution to get rid of the obsessive images was to get some pay back time with them, either by sending them angry mail, email, saying evil prayer for them.

Then my mind switched back to reality Peter Son told "by certain time said, for example 10, 12, 4, 6 p.m. those are the times we need to pull the items from the shelf, put it in the cart, people working out on the sales floor will roll it out.

Inside the stock room imaged me in a 21 century battle field. Fritz, Big Sean, Little Sean, Peter Son, Frank, Lamont, we were similar to modern day warrior, only weapon was our hand held electronic device, batteries inside considered to be our source of ammunition.

I could hear the Big Chief Bob from the other side of the room, giving the order, "o.k. the customer waiting for the order, please don't screw up." "Big Sean, you work on the trailer, Little Sean, you take the pet items, Frank, take care of the bed, toy, Fritz, work on the pillow, bed and chemical, Peter Son, please stay close with Johnny, since his the new kid on the block, give a chance, because he doesn't what the hell his doing?" Bob commanded.

I recalled one Saturday, either in August or July; one or two guys called in sick. It was only me and Bob, running the show, dropping the café, from our gun and pulling the items from the shelf, for next three to four hours, we were like robot, both sweating like an angry dog.

In any retail business, no matter what, the customer always come first, they were usually right, considered bad blood to start an argument, never cruse at the clients, result could be termination, if they needed something it wasn't good policy to kept them waiting for a long period of time.

The sale manager, the stock people working on that day were getting excited and very anxious. They kept complaining to Bob, "What's taking so long in getting the orders out?" They asked. "The customer needs it right away!" They demanded.

Me and Bob, doing our best, out of his compassion, kindness didn't said a word to me, instead he's real piss off with the manager above him. He just said "just tell them they have no other choice, but to be patient, we're doing our best to get the merchandise out, is only me and Johnny, his doing a hell of job."

Finally by 4 o' clock Little Sean came in with his imagery fire truck, brought out the holes, to put out the burning flame. Boy was I glad to see him, he saved our teeth.

Some night, when I felt for Bob and Sean, it was between the both of them, they had to drop a couple of café, pulled a huge number of stuff to the sale floor.

Those times, I stayed with Little Sean and Peter Son to give them some help. Some situation, could tell Sean seem a little upset, when I explained to him, needed to catch the Nassau County bus, which only comes at every half an hour. As days gone by, he begins to slowly understand, traveling from Hicksville to Flushing, a rather very long trip, if one didn't own a car.

As a good gesture, some nights, offered to assist Peter Son. There was usually a big smile on his face. I highly respected him, never gave me the heavy load or things to high to reach, if it happen to beyond my reach.

His motto was "Johnny you must come first before any things else." After our job was over, when we headed toward the Human Resources Office, often jokes about the Mets and Yankees with him, usually told him "the Mets possessed a better team, because their player represented the city of New York, while the Yankees don't give a damn, instead to me, they're very selfish, collected big bonuses, carrying a fat wallet stuff with million of dollars inside, always mentioned to him "the Mets will beat the Yankees in the World Series, if they ever meet." His respond was "oh yeah Johnny we're see."

I always admired all those guys in the back stock room. Frank was a martial art expect. He knew everything concerning Bruce Lee, Jackie Chan, and Jet Lee. He told me "Bruce Lee was the best, he's the legend, no one could compare to him." He liked Jackie Chan, saying "he's a funny character."

Before I moved on to another position in the store, I explained to those guys "this was back in 1977 before all you were born, I went to Thomas Edison High School, about 95% Blacks, and I was the only Chinese duce.

They said "Johnny, Johnny you know that duce Bruce Lee, did he beat up the Black duce Jim Kelly?" They asked me. "You Johnny Bruce Lee is not dead, he's still alive, his hiding somewhere, when he comes back to life, his going to be the Black Bruce Lee."

Afterward they all started to laugh crazy. They could stop laughing for over 5 minutes, though it was a real cool joke. Somehow I considered all of those guys as Chinese Soul Brother. In some way, they all looked after me. Even good old Bob stick out his life for me.

I recalled one summer day, when all of NYC was flooded; most of the people couldn't relied on public transportation to get to work. I started calling to Target at 6, 6:30, 6:45 p.m. about 4 times, no one answer, finally I tried at 10:30, Alice the receptionist said I didn't called, so she put me down for "no show, no call" on my employment record. When I tired to explain everything to her, she' kind of angry, kept telling me, "everybody who couldn't made it call, except you."

From that point on, knew dealing with a very angry person, not very pleasant, so I spoke with Bob on the phone, he explained to me "you have absolutely nothing to worry about Johnny, just ignored what Alice said." "When you come in tomorrow, I have everything taken care of, o.k." The next day on the job, told me "he's taken cared of everything, I wouldn't be on record. "Well that just a real treat from a very cool fellow, I wish every boss in Target will be like Bob." I said to myself.

Little Sean might be pretty sneaky and wise, but there duce, normally look out for me. He warned me about climbing ladder, telling me to be extremely careful picking up heavy boxes. Once I cut myself with a blank accidentally, I tried ignoring the pain telling him "is only small cut, the bleeding." His response, "no didn't wanted to let germs go into my finger, you could get infected, please go to human resources, asked for a band aid."

The other day, they posted everybody score on the wall. I happen to be the last guy on the list. As soon as Bob, came in, he said to me "don't be afraid, not a thing to worry over, his going to work with me." I let Peter Son knew, "hey I afraid, I might be out of a job, because I scored 88, needed to score 95 percent accuracy in pulling the products. "From now on, just watch and worked with me." He said.

Once or twice, when we had to pull the products from the shelf, I had to move a lot of the boxes out of the way, in order to scan the bar code. As soon as he came over, shaking his head, embarrassing in front of the other guys, "come on Johnny, you wasn't a lot of time, could of moved to a less crowded location." He said. I answered angrily to him "why can you just come down, can't help it, there's too many boxes and they're very heavy to move by one person."

Another time I wasn't consecrating on the job, was thinking girls in one-piece swimsuit in the shopping mall pool, I scan the bar code outside the carton, took some stuff out, forgot the number of counts and I told him. "You got to consecrate on what you doing." He said. "Hey I am doing the best I could." I said. "If that the best you could do, then that's fine." He said. Later on we took a glance at each other and started to smile, he laughed, shaking his head. I could read his mind, guess it said "this guy Johnny got to stop thinking about girls in general and consecrate on his work."

The next morning at work, in for a shock. Omar introduced me to a new Black fellow named Brian. Since I had an illness, didn't knew what to do or expect, just froze there for a couple of second. He was quite, didn't wanted to shake my hand. It was to be my first real test, a Black, not begin friendly or nice to me.

Omar told me to work with him; I had him doing the back stock. When the boxes were falling down from the tub, he just stood there and watches me picking it up, didn't even brother to ask me if he could help to grab the fallen carton with his hand. "Boy this guy not very nice." Said to myself, didn't even said a word to me. Finally I asked him "can you please give me a hand with the boxes."

Before I showed him how to point the gun at the label to scan the order number, he said to me he knew how to use the already. When Little Sean and some of the other fellow came in, he's started to socialize with them. I can't read his mind, was it racism he had toward Asian, was it begin shy and quite.

This wasn't going too well, loosing the battle. For the next couple of days, tired my best to avoid him, whenever his working on the top floor, I'll went down stair, if his next to me, went somewhere else, pretty sure of you heard that familiar expression, the harder you tried to avoid a particular individual, most likely, they will cross your path, meaning more than 90% of the time, you're going to run into that person.

First time, I meet him; he struck me out, by throwing a nasty screw ball, nasty curved ball and a split finger fast ball. Here I am in a lousy situation, a Black person giving me the cold shoulder.

The old saying "Blacks are everywhere on planet Earth, that is totally true, even going to the Asian countries, in Hong Kong during 1992, not many, I saw in the tourist section. Even in China nowadays, there are Blacks studying to learn to speak, read, write Chinese, some resided in Hong Kong, China, holding high government jobs.

The next time, I confronted him, tried to sweet talk, be nice to him. I said to him "he might be racist against Chinese People, was still going to be his friend and if he had question, could come to me for assistance.

It turned out to be the worst moved. He counter moved by using his Queen to corner trapped my king, putting me in a dangerous position. He held the upper hand, in a good position. It was check on me, no other choice, but to move my King out of position. I though of using harsh verbal remarks, tap him in the arm or shoulder. I remember that how I loose jobs in the past. This occasion, wasn't going to create the same error, didn't wanted history to repeat itself.

Life was always a learning experience. I comprehended the hard facts. People who are very racist, if they didn't want to associate with others, then let it be, you can't force them. If the person made a racist remarks, physically, verbally aggressive, then bring it up to your supervisor. If he or she said "oh let it go they're only playing with you." Then reported to Human Resources, if they too decided not to act, go to upper channel, meaning brining a lawsuit, most individual don't understand racist and sexual remarks, most manager don't take it lightly, is a very serious matter.

On the other hand, a person had to understand working in blue-collar dead-end job, very low paid, especially in warehouses, receiving docks, racism, bigotry, sexual remarks very common, just needed to have a little tolerates.

I experiences in every job, there's always one or two jackasses, cannot be good friends, bubby, bubby, with everybody, not all individuals possessed well manner, friendly, nice geyser. The main objective come in, do your own work, if able to, then give co-worker a hand.

Someday, I bumped into Bob in the break room. One day I saw him reading a book, had no idea, if a war novel. I showed him, I purchased a World War 11 aircraft carrier book.

He told me he "served in Vietnam." I asked him "what rifle the troops used during the war." He said "the M-16." I mentioned to him "problem with the M-16, it jammed sometime, meaning the gun won't open fire, cost the lives of many servicemen. I told him "during the second World War, the M-1 Carbine, the U.S. army standard, best rifle. He said "if a person got hit by an M-1 rifle bullet, hoping to survive was a very slim margin.

Then both of us brought up a funny comment, during the Korea War, when U.S. Forces were shooting invading Chinese Armies, they came like human waves. The American 50 caliber machine gun, need to be cooled by water, so I asked him, "What happen w hen there's no water to cool the gun?" He said "the solider standing in front of the gun, urinated on it." Afterward we both started laughing. What made it even funnier; he said "is no joke, which is the absolute truth to the story.

As we headed back to the stock room, he said "Johnny you are no longer doing back room stock, you're going to be out on the sale floor, doing zoning." "Oh is easier than back room stock, just pick up all the loose items, use your gun to scan and place it in it proper location." "Well I am going to miss you Bob, you are a good guy." I said. "Don't worry Johnny, I'll be around, I am not going no places, I'll be here, you're see me." "Go to Ronald in H R he'll have your schedule."

I am going to miss those guys and Bob in the back stock; they were a great bunch of guys. Once I explained to Little Sean and Fritz, "the problem with most people they too hyper on the job, don't know how to relax a little, nothing wrong in making monies." "The most importance thing is your health, no matter how much monies, you have in your account, when a person dies, can't take the monies to their grave." They agreed with me and started to laugh. I went on to said "life is very short, we don't know how much time, we have on Earth, maybe after work, catching my bus, I can go out and get run over by a car and that will be the end of me, in life everybody need to have a little sense of humor, because life is very short indeed." "You hit it right on the nail, Johnny Quest, give me five." Little Sean said.

I hated to take the N20 bus. It is always crowded. I remember every morning, no matter how early I woke up, by the time I get to the station, there's about more than ten people waiting on line ahead of me. Even by 5:30 a.m. it was crowded already, coming back to Flushing packed, very dense like Sardine can.

Some of the bus driver were pretty nice, then some consider to be nasty, rule, cruel, couldn't care less to answer your question, like the folks who worked for the MTA mass transit, they carried this attitude, the general public owe them something.

Somehow I was sick and tired of these people attitude, about two or three times a week, they get into a physical, verbal confrontation with each other, due to the limited of space in the vehicle.

Most of the individual who took the vehicle were mainly Blacks, Latinos and Asians. One occasion, bumped into a Black fellow, whose occupation was a security guard? I got out of Target at a late Saturday afternoon to my surprise, waiting for the N20, three or four buses passes by, not a single N20 came by, this need looked good, getting nervous, butter flies in my stomach, felt like begin stranded out in Long Island, so I approached this person, spoke to me nicely, "there's no N20 after a certain time on the weekend, you need to catch one of these bus, which would take you to Clock Tower Roslyn, from there, take the N21, leaved you off directly at Main Street, Flushing.

Afterward, we struck up an interesting conversation; we agreed who White folks keep move out of the cities. We said Blacks and minorities moved out to the suburb also. He said "escaping the problem, never the best solution, must learn to deal with the issues, because no matter where you go, the problem is going to be with the person." He said "there is public transportation, which will take minorities and poor folks to the suburbs." I asked him "where you live?" He said "Great Neck." "You must be very rich, you know how much, the houses cost over there." "No I am not rich at all; I need to have two jobs in order to make end meets." "The more I earned the more Uncle Sam takes away from my paid check." "Well you know the familiar expression in America there's no free lunch." I said and he started to laugh. I explained "whiled at Queens College my professor said "poor folks, minorities getting government grants to pay for their tuition, but once they graduated, if found a job, no matter who you are, couldn't get away, must paid taxes to Uncle Sam, that's what we meant, by no free lunch in America."

We hopped on the bus to Clock Tower, discussed about how the wealthy individuals living in Long Island, the expensive property taxes were paying for the school system and city planning. As the vehicle approached Great Neck, we mentioned "farewell to each other." Well another good day at Target Hicksville.

I was off to my new job, the next day, and zoning. It wasn't a glamorous job, kind of boring, lousy, waste of time. On the other hand, felt like a tank commander, over seeing the front line of the battlefield. Imaged myself in a war game, when taking loose merchandise on the floor, it was like removing land mines on the battlefield.

One day I didn't had my name tag on, Mitch the store manager wasn't too happy, he question me "where your name tag?" I answered him "I left it home." "Please go to Human Resources and put one on, is importance for you to have a name tag." He mentioned.

I like Mitch, I think his a very cool manager, if a person was slow, didn't picked things up right away, he didn't get on that person case. If you were new to the department, he had compassion, understanding.

Sometime when it wasn't too busy, countered some interesting conversation with him in the break room. I said "you must be a very wealthy man, being the store manager." "No not really Johnny, the cost of living is very high in Nassau County, property taxes are tremendously high." "What kind of job you had, before you employed with Target?" I asked him. "I used to have my own business." "What kind of business?" "We manufactured clothing and tie." "Was it a big market; did you made a lot of money off it?" "It was fair, some period, did well, at times, similar to many enterprise, considered to be slow." He's one cool executive, even during his break, I recalled, one day, needed to speak to Ron from receiving, he was having a cup of coffee with Jennifer, felt kind of shocked, told me to pull up a chair and asked me "how could he help me."

I memorized all the guys in zoning. In the electronic department, I believed Rich, the leader of the pack. Finny, a super cool duce with Marvin and Luis, nicknamed Luis the Latino Playboy, once Anna who worked for Stark buck was laughing her head off. That was occasion, when so busy with my work, Luis will say "Johnny you didn't say hi or good morning to me." "I am so sorry Luis, I just forgotten, it won't happen next time." "You better be, Johnny, there's no excuse you're in my department." I knew he was only joking, wanted to be a wise character.

Out of the blue, one day he brought lunch for me. Whenever we were on our break, wished to repay him by purchasing a soda, potatoes chips, he will always turned it down. Wow in my heart, when I view this person, who really have the heart of giving, without expecting anything in return. A real true heart, he possessive it, in most business environment when an employee help out one another, a person expect something from each other, said for an exampled, a co-worker purchased a cup of coffee or lunch there's exchange of favorite, but not in the case of Luis, later on in life, he taught me the true gift of giving from the heart.

One of the major difficulty of zoning was you could never get your work done. The difficult of being out on the sale floor was you had to deal with the customer. In every retail service, no matter what, they were, your first priorities, didn't matter how demanding they expressed, we had to tend to their needs.

Since I was still new to the store, a feeling of embarrassment, did knew where to direct the client, for example when one customer asked me a question, before I could answered their question, another would dropped by to ask me where certain stuff be located at.

There was a cool duce named Sonny, a really big help to me. He answered most of the customer question, why I didn't, where, how to direct them. I was working in Blue World, which consisted of electronic, toys, gardens, power tools, automotive, camping, equipments, school supplies, videos and c d.

Later on I learned the trick, electronic arranged in the alphabet E section, toys, games in G section, school, home supplies were in H or R sector, videos, and c d were situated in C and D areas.

There was a very pretty intern named Judy these were the advice she gave to me. She's a very nice person; sometime handled a few items on a cart load of stuffs pushed it to the floor. Her comment "Johnny I am not rushing you, don't worry about making errors, please if you're not sure, just asked one of the employee."

"Wow what a nice and sweet thing to say, coming from a pretty girl." I said to myself. There was about two to three occasion, I didn't take my full 45 minutes and she saw me going into the break room, she's followed me, told me "Johnny you forgot to take your full 45 lunch break. "I am sorry, sometime when is too busy, I often forget." I said. "That's perfectly o.k. I understand." She said.

That was the final time, I saw, spoke to her. She was an intern, stayed with us for about ten weeks. You know they were college students, employed for the summer, so could paid their tuition, upon graduation, they're promised for an executive position with Target.

It was sad to see Judy left, happened to be one of the best L.O.D., stands for leader of department, well like they said "autumn leaves must fall, September came, and school, just around the corner for a lot of these young kids. What could I said, she's varnished into the divine wind.

Zoning wasn't working out for me, majority of co-workers knew right away where most of the products where they belong to. I was not very productive in this area of work; somehow I tried my best to place things in their proper order. I don't exactly remember, but got some wonderful comments from co-workers and manager that I picked things up from the floor. Some days there were no re-shop meaning putting stuffs according to their department sections, so very slow.

From those periods on, looked forward in having the 45 lunch and 10 minutes break, usually bumped into Finny in the break room, conversation happened to be very interesting, of course most discussion center on women. I spoke to him "some girls in Target got a bad, nasty attitude, young idiot real immature." He definitely agreed with me. On the other hand, one or a couple of bad apple won't spoil the whole bunch. We said "there were some fine women in Target." One thing I admired Finny statement he didn't think dating with a female co-workers, considered the wildest thing to do in any working environment. He said "whatever you do within the company, when it came to business, put it in perspective."

One thing I had comparison with him, while many kids graduated from high school around the age of 17, 18. Me and didn't graduated until at the age of 20. We both struggled with Basic English and Math. I told him, used to cheat in school. He gave me a dose of good laugh, mentioned "could care less." I assumed, probably did the same stuff.

I clarified to him in one situation, around 1984, in a retail department store, used to be called Alexander, I just completed an employment application, guessed what interview said to me "oh Mr. Wong you're behind." She was very noisy. "What do your parents do for living?" She asked. My answered was "my father worked in the Chinese restaurant and my mom employed in the garment district." "Well the government gave you the opportunities to go to school." She said. Nowadays if any interviewer asked me those question, I'll said to them "that not a very nice thing to say and is really none of your business what my parent do for a living."

He definitely agreed with me, saying "they did the same crap to him." "Every one in Target let's all said three cheers for Finny, three cheers for him indeed." I said. Unfortunately, he mentioned "there are those who in authority figure, abuse, say ridicule stuffs to give individual low self-esteem, they enjoy abusing their power over peoples.

His answer was absolutely right from my past working experiences, I saw it all the times. The way I see, we all want to get ahead in life, absolutely nothing wrong in aiming for a promotion, getting more monies, on the contrary let's not do it in a way to step on other employees shoes or abuse your authorities to make yourself look good in front of upper managers.

Then there are those workers who loved to kiss other people or manager asses in order to get ahead and please themselves. These individuals are very selfish, don't concern about helping others, but assisting themselves. They are not doing for the interest of others, only looking out for their own.

Comes September, children's, teenagers, adults returned to school. Older men, women, reported back to work. The autumn season was probably one of the saddest calendar periods of the year.

The warm gentle cool summer breeze, no longer communicates to us, instead the cruel, angry wind of autumn comes knocking on our doorstep. It carried a message of anxieties, because at this moment in our life, either being successful in school or in our career.

I had fond memories when returning back to school was considered one of the most depressing periods of my life. Nobody wanted to look forward to six hours situated in a building, while going back home, there were homework and exam to be studied.

In college one's repeated the same boredom life of elementary, junior and high school. The college bright spot with university life, you get to choose what's your major, enjoyed your study, but it wasn't an easy case, you had to pick an academic where if you go into, there will be employment opportunities.

Contrast to secondary education, college, if you're not Black or minorities, there weren't any financial aid you could qualify. The only bright spot if the school provided scholarship, if not a person needed to relied heavy on student loan, which is 8% interest rate, must be paid back six months upon graduation. I remember during 1987, borrowed around 1,500 dollars to attend New York Tech. in Old Westbury Long Island, never finished the program, and dropped out, next year received over a hundred mails, demanding I paid back the loan.

I could see Target was gearing for the fall season. A large section of school supplies, being delivered to the back stock room, consisted of books, pens, pencils, notebooks, lose leafs sheets, magic markers, crayons, rulers, protractors, inks, may be some text books.

Summer clothing's such as shorts, swimsuits, short sleeves shirts were being pulled off from the shelf, being placed with long sleeves shirts, dress pants, dress suits for women, two piece suit for men, working shoes and finally designer jeans.

Also appeared in the picture, arrival of new employees, couldn't remember any of their names, but most of them were very pleasant, greeted them, having short conversation.

Somehow felt we were soldiers of employees getting ready to meet the demand of many clients, yet our nation economy was collapsing, due to the over spending on the Iraq war. I didn't knew, how much capital or monies was in the American wallet. I had some beliefs our beloved nation was loosing jobs as years approached. We were building fortress of meeting the customer satisfaction.

The next day Ron from Human Resources asked me to come into his office for a chant. I was very nervous, as soon as he told me what happened, my kneed and body shaking rapidly, hoping he wasn't going to give me the ax, can me, beside I might be slower than the average person, madding huge mistakes, I always answered the call by working hard as any body else. I felt my throat real tight, body very tense, noticed some employee greeted me, so tense, could hardly breath, and opened my mouth to say "hi."

By 10 a.m. arrived at his office. He greeted me, "hi Johnny, how's everything, please tell me how are you doing?" He asked. I was so shocked by his pleasant statement, though; he might be saying "how come things aren't working out?" "I been hearing reports, you haven't been consecrating, not producing well in your work." No one of those words directed at me, instead he was interesting in seeing if I needed any accommodation.

"I heard you have a disability, is quite o.k. you have full confidentiality, I won't leaked this information to anybody." "Are you possibly sure about this, because if you do, I will be out of a job." "Could you please guarantee you're kept it shut to the L.O.D. leaders of departments?" "Please don't worry Johnny, you have absolutely nothing to worry about, you're have my full guarantee."

"There's an opening in the freezer, frozen goods department, will you be interesting?" "Alright no problems, how flexible are you, could you arrived around 6:45 or 7:00 a.m. in the morning at the receiving dock?" "No sweat at all." I just needed to wake up a little earlier." "There's not too much stress or thinking involved, you just needed to make sure, putting the food in its proper place." "Please report to Ron in receiving his very nice person." "If you don't pick things up right away, or a bit too slow, he's very understanding, he won't yell, scream, and get on your nerve." "I am afraid that will be all, are there any question, if not, I wish you the best of luck, Johnny." "Thank very much." As I was exiting the Human Resources, lo and behold, guessed who I bumped into, none other than Ron himself? "Hey Johnny did you spoke to Ron of H R?" "Yes, I just did." "How about working in the freezer, frozen goods department, most of the guys are o.k. if you don't understand or have any question, please asked, we will be more than happy to help you Johnny."

Before I headed off to the frozen goods department, decided to purchased a candy bar. At first was frighten to go to a Black cashier, so I said "I have nothing to loose, if they weren't friendly or nice to me, then God please let me not say any harsh, angry words to them, let me ignore them and walk away."

"Hi Johnny, how are you, that's all you buying?" She asked. I could tell by her accent, she's Jamaican. "You know, I am going to call you Johnny Carson, from now on." She said. "Well good luck to you, because Johnny Carson is dead, no longer around." I said. "In that case you could be the Chinese Johnny Carson." She said. Afterward we started to laugh. It turned out her name was Sophie.

During my stay in Target, she was considered somewhat a mother figure. I was very happy, she considered herself to be a Christian, really admired her faith in the bible, her walk with the Lord, her words of encouragement, she poured on me, during difficulties in my life. She's usually happy, very spiritually, very up lifting.

"I told her "some of the harsh things I did in life and having a vengeance heart." "It doesn't matter Johnny God still loves you, he's died for your sins, I am glad you're honest with him." She said. "Well I don't think God will honor a person like me, who said evil prayer wishing those who's hurt me to perish in a car accident." I said. "Johnny God knows our heart, we are not perfect, when we failed, we must confess our sins, and he's forgiving us." There was time, I was so upset with certain individuals back in Kansas

City, couldn't consecrate at my work and I would said to her "Sophie please don't tell me, how much God loves me, because I am suffering so much." She's have that pleasant smile on her face and said "Johnny don't worry, you're be o.k. I pray for you."

Later on I introduced myself to Terrace. He was a wise crack funny duce, pretty friendly individual. He told me "we get delivery on Mondays, Wednesdays, and Fridays." They arrived around 7 a.m. in the morning." He said.
He showed me where the cooler located right next to the freezer. "The yoga, milk, dairy products belonged in the cooler, while ice-cream, frozen foods stayed in the freezer." He also taught me certain way to pull the skit. Those skids were loaded with goods and they were very heavy indeed. Friday, the worst day of them all, we got the most delivery on that day, we got butter, juice, yoga, ice-cream, meats, frozen foods, milks, Jell-O, eggs, cheese, you name them, everything came on Friday.

We got a great crew in this department, Tim, Chris, John, Ray. Terrance put me in charge of the yoga, Jell-O, eggs, juices and cheeses. Chris a college duce, this job happen to be his bread and butter, needed to pay for his tuition, beside working at Target, his other employment was in the movie theater by the mall, by the time he finished working through the day, felt like passing out, because put in an average of 13 hours a day.

He's goes to Stony Brook University in Long Island, still pretty decent college, the only difficulty, he resided on campus, many nights, no sleep, because they turned on the loud music, similar to blasting the stereo to full volume.

I often refer Chris as Superman; he looks in some way, like Christopher Reeves. Chris was your typical all-American kid; he symbolized the American work-ethic. There his willing to tackle any job, going to school during the fall season. He remained me some of the past New York Senator while during the summer, they labored tremendously numbers of hours, comes September head off to school/

Tim, a great teenager, high school, cool duce, me and him usually had one or two good jokes in regard to certain group of women and race of people. A slimly character told me, "Johnny do the best you could, don't take any crap from anybody."

John, a wise guy character, who often possessed a funny joke, if he didn't like certain employees, he blasted, criticizing them, giving them a bad rap. Somehow I and he were a great team; he taught me everything, the ins and outs, the rope in the department, the do's and don'ts.

In the frozen section, I consider him, the leader of the pack. He was big, but had a gigantic heart for people, never condemned me for not putting certain foods away fast enough. Whenever a client asked me "if we carried anything on stock", he will be more than happy to assist them. He took real care of me, making sure nobody burst my chops. He won't let anybody to get on Johnny Wong case.

It was fun, stocking the shelf with items. Some occasion, laboring as reverently, you felt a hunger in your stomach, so once glanced at the frozen cuisine, imaged myself, only if Target had a microwave, let me popped one up and just globed down as quickly as possible.

Looking at those cuisines remained me of the cooking show entitled "the Iron Chef." Some circumstances though of I as being a chef at Target, cooking to the L.O.D. team leaders and employees. Imaging myself swinging the knifes, flipping the pots and pans, cooking the meals, decorating a cheese cake, "wow viewing myself going up to the stand, receiving "the Iron Chef" trophy.

I loved putting away the yoga. Terrance ordered a lot of them, especially during the summer, people enjoyed eating them. Twice a week, they were on sale, another items that go on sale was the juice. We carried a variety of orange juice, the frozen vegetables sea food cuisine another hot product, people normally purchased. During the summer, the ice-cream crowded the receiving dock, customers like buying the pizzas if on sale.

There was time, the delivery people came from bran named company. When stocking the bread, ice-cream, we had a good conversation between us, some situation presented humor jokes, normally spoke mainly on sports. Baseball was the name of the game, we usually discussed among ourselves, very happy those fellow symbolized the good luck charm, almost every single one happen to be a gun-ho Mets New York Mets fan, boy that really made my days go by quicker.

Which group of people, I consider the worst, even though, had many bad experiences with Blacks, my own personal opinion, the Chinese was the worst at Target, especially the customers. In one situation I was brushing my teeth in the bathroom, because I just finished eating my dinner. As I was brushing, this Chinese old man noticed it, kept on staring at me. I glanced back at him; he won't turn his eyes away from me. We were at a staring match; I assumed he won the contest, because he waited for me to turn my head away from him. Another scenario one Chinese women, looking at the yoga stack, I asked her "can I help you find something?" She totally ignored me. The other time, moving the garbage cart, I told her to "watch her back, she won't moved her shopping cart, so I didn't really had enough room to maneuver, the garbage cart hit her shopping cart slightly. One time, I was putting away some frozen foods, next thing, as I turned around this woman tried to trash some of the Target frozen meats to the garbage cage. I said "please don't do that, that not very nice." She asked me if I could have the shopping cart." She's holding two carbine bins. I explained to her, "We needed to dump the empty carton." "You could obtain one near the parking exit." She won't go away, until she had the shopping cart, finally I gave in to her demand. Guess what? I found it hard to believe, she mentioned two simple words of "thank you", to me. Even to this very day, as I am writing my manuscript, I still find it hard, coming from a Chinese person.

Friday was the worst day for me. Most of the day, I am alone by myself, moving those skids, they were heavy as hell. Some of the employees were nice enough to help me moved the skids. They're pushed the back, while I dragged the heavy load.

One day, Gina noticed, I was struggling, out of all the women in Target; she's the only one who asked me "if I was o.k.?" Somehow those words meant more to me than the physical assistance, but now, please don't get me wrong, I am always happy on whoever could help me to move those skids. When she asked that, she's worry, showed some sort of concern for me.

Words could be very strong, hold tremendous impact, if used in negative term, will totally destroyed a person emotionally, vice versa, Gina words was showing care and kindness.

I always like Gina, she just possessed this personalities where, she plain, right down friendly, happy to be around co-workers, never saw her once, ever having any angry words with any clients, managers or employees. Maybe once I said "hi" to her, no responded from her. Another situation, she said "thank you Johnny", I didn't responded the first time, she repeated again and I answered her "You're welcome."

When I viewed her attributes there's a message in my mind, "Johnny, you might had many bad experiences with Blacks, I perfectly understand how you felt, but not all Blacks are bad, condemned criminals, we're just like normal individuals struggling financially, in the same boat as you, not perfect people, sometime we could be nice, we have our rough times, if going through a bad day, similar to anybody else on this planet.

I think I got to know Gina, when I was zoning the department, often clients approached me with a question concerning the location of certain products, right away, encountered the goose bump, right away, and she didn't hesitated to answer their question for me.

When I was pulling items in the back stock room, nobody ever really thanked me for putting their stuff in the cart, she's always thanked me. I tired my best to help other, as I was throwing my own garbage. When I saw employees coming in with cartons, usually asked them, if could offered my assistance in trashing their garbage. Some took advantage of me, even if they had a little trash in their cart, they're still let me throw their trash in the dumpster. That was not the case with Gina, when I offered to help her, she's said "that o.k. thanks you very much, very nice and sweet of you, I only have a little." When I left target, I was glad I had a friend like Gina. I am very glad; she's the type of person that I knew.

That was a duce named Sam. I don't know much about him but it seems he was a real happy jolly fellow, going around smiling laughing and cracking jokes. I liked to be around him, he made the day go by a little quicker. One major fault he possessed, one lazy duce.

"Ha, ha, Johnny I heard you were in the Chinese Tong." He said. "What's the Tong?" "Is the Chinese gangster?" "Oh yeah, that so stupid of me, how can I missed that." At times I said to him "you know the Chinese and the Jews, the hardest workers, the best people on Earth." "Yeah you're right on that Johnny, give me five." "The Jewish people are the number one fan of Chinese food; you folks give us more than a million bucks a year." "Of course Johnny, I couldn't think of any one who didn't like Chinese foods." "I have it about twice a week, especially when I get paid."

Then one day the unexpected happen. I was caught off balance; fell off from the safety net. On that particular Friday, all by me needed his assistance to pull the heavy skid. Normally on a Friday, I get an average of about 4 to 5 skids, made a request and he promised me, but failed to keep his words. As I was pulling the last skid, he showed at the wrong time and asked me "if I needed his help." No Sam that o.k." I responded angrily. Boy, erupting like red hot volcanoes. "Johnny, Terrance is going to get piss off at me; he's going to ask me, how Johnny is doing today by himself." "I am going to give you Luis for the time being."

On this day the crap really hit the fan. The freezer was already crowded with dairy products and goods, trying to get the final skid to the freezer, but to no avail. The way our manufacturer put the yoga, jell-o, cheese, meats at a bad position. As I was wheeling in the frozen goods, all of a sudden, the yoga started to fall down on the floor. I told Luis, "I am going to get some napkins and cleaned up the mess."

Then later on, I didn't know, he probably saw Luis standing there all by himself. "Johnny how come, I saw Luis standing there, doing nothing?" Boy was I mad as hell. "What the hell you mean you saw Luis standing there doing nothing?" "Do you know that the yoga spilled on the floor, I had to get some paper napkins to wipe the stuff?" "Beside you saw Luis standing there, he doesn't know anything about our department, and I had to explain to him what to do." "Come down, Johnny, just come down, you don't need to be defensive with me." "I am not trying to be defensive, you don't understand the facts, and I am just trying to tell you."

A couple of minutes, he returned, this time with compassionate words. "Johnny nobody is saying you were lazy, not doing your job, nobody is criticizing you, from what I observed and other people, you're doing a great job." "Thank you very much, I am very sorry, if I hurt your feeling, please let me buy you a soda." "I wanted to make up for it." "I don't desired bad blood or harsh feeling between us." "No that perfectly o.k. Johnny, no problem at all, you're fine."

Afterward I never had any hard feeling with Sam, don't think I ever asked him for help, might have, but didn't had high expectation on him. Sam to my opinion was not an evil, cruel person that would challenge you to a physical confrontation. The way I viewed people for ever if they performed anger action, there usually a soft side in he or she, I mean he did came back apologize, spoke some good words to me. The only difficulty was he didn't really take his job seriously. The things I saw in him, he was your average bar person in the crowd, loved to hang out in the bar, created a few jokes, and have a drink, share your laughter.

I needed to be honest with almost everybody in Target. I felt kind of good when he got can from the exec. But later I viewed myself as a total hypocrite, in the past, I said evil, angry, cursing at other, gossiping behind other people back, what right do I had to feel good for Sam, if I label myself a Christian, even having hate and negative words against him, considered to be wrong in the sight of God.

A couple days when I left Target, decided to pray for Sam. "Please God provide him a job, times are hard, there's a lot of people out of work." "He couldn't continue to live out of his saving." "Is going to empty out as time flew by, as time went by I also had loving remorse and pity for Sam.

During the 1962 Cuban Missiles crisis, even to this day, I'll always cherished Kennedy speech, didn't recalled what the exact quote was. "We are all immortal, we live on planet Earth. "Somehow we must learn to cherish and learned to share the resources on this planet or we're perished."

I had some great news for everybody in Target. From now, I am going to get a ride early in the morning, none other than my college bubby. The one and only David Fool Man Chug, I desired the whole wide world would know David Dixon. We go back, when we were at Newtown high school. He was in my Earth

110   *Johnny Wong*

Science class. The way he answered the teacher question, it seem like coming from a Nobel Prize person. Each respond contained a mathematical solution. I foreshadow his future, imaged one day he would be a Harvard professor teaching chemistry, physics, biology and earth science. Someday he probably mentioned "well Mr. Wong why you always daydreaming about girls, why can't you consecrate on my lecture just for once." "When you don't succeed, you have nobody to blame, but yourself." He quoted.

We hooked up with each other, while in Queens's borough Community College. I was so shocked to see him there. A real genius like him, why he's doing in a two year college, he told me "he wanted first to get his associate, then later on, go to a four year university to get his bachelor degree.

We found each other in the Agape Christian Fellowship. Every Wednesday afternoon from 12-2 p.m., was club hours, a great bunch of people, super time for sharing, studying the scriptures, reading the bible together and praying with one another. I recalled the first time, we went there, and a fellow by the name Paul introduced himself to me and David.

The scariest moment in the fellowship was one day, they showed, "The Thief of the Night." Is based on a character named Patty, she's heard the Gospel many occasion, was relying on her feeling, refused to make a decision for Christ. One evening her husband accepted Christ in his heart. That night she had a dream where the rapture Christian went up to heaven to meet their savior and she was left behind. When she woke up, her dream became a reality. I recalled seeing that film, my junior year of high school.

When it came to English composition, essay I was suck, never gave a sucker an easy break like me. No doubt about, he was like a relief pitcher who came out of the bullpen to proof read my essay. Similar to a college professor full with all these wonderful details, similes, metaphor, the way he written, correcting was poetic in action. The way he checking the error, similar to dropping pipe bombs on the paper.

Today happened to be my first ride to Target Hicksville, kind of special feeling, early dawn in the morning, sometime popped into my the Beatle song "Black Bird sinning at the crack of dawn." A great feeling seeing the moon some morning, we spoke about the atmosphere on the moon, is very cold in the morning, while in the afternoon, it gets extremely hot, that why astronaut wear spacesuit.

Imaged David Fool Man Chug car as a rocket, New York City was Earth bound, Hicksville Long Island was situated on the moon. Stars represented the traffic light; felt we were marching, gearing for combat mission.

Since this was our first mission on the road, he had a little hard time finding where Hicksville was. Yesterday I went to the mall, handled him a map of Hicksville. I told him Hicksville was either on exit 42 or 49. We finally got there around 6:40 in front of Broadway mall. I tired to get in; I could believed it, happen to be lock, "good now I am going to be late at work, how I am going to enter Target." I said to myself.

Then suddenly somewhere out of the Blue, a long rancher, a Black state trooper, "I probably believed you worked for one of the retail store at the mall and you are trying to get in, don't worry just hop on over to my car, have a seat, made yourself comfortable." He said. "Wow boy was I glad to see you, you just save my life." I said. "Please tell the name of the store you worked for, so I could give you a ride." He asked.

I thank the state trooper and headed for Target, to myself, noticed the gates close, so I tried my best to find an employee, then, noticed Toni, putting away some stuff on the shelf, she spotted and told me "to go to the side door, I think she opened the door to let me in.

Unfortunately I had to deal with Alice, usually a pain in the rear end. I had to explained to her my schedule wasn't with the Zoning department, but with the freezer. "What is these Johnny, how come, you don't tell me or notify me, if you're not on the schedule, how you expect to get paid, and am I being reasonable." She said angrily.

"Well this woman must probably have a lot of personal issues and she's bringing it to work, what a way to start the day off, by raising her voice at me." I said to myself.

I spotted Abdul and started a conversation with him, told him "why his wasting his time in Target?" To my knowledge, he went to Queens College also, I graduated in June 1985, I recalled he started to attend somewhere around 1998, but never finished. He said "he was a computer science major, didn't complete. Is importance to finish your college education, without a college degree was impossible to find a decent job nowadays? I gave him a couple of website to search on the internet. I clarified to him "the MTA New York City Transit was hiring and the Long Island Railroad. He let me knew, he's trying to get his commercial vehicle license.

People who are nice like Abdul; I don't mind extending a helping hand to him. My belief was you could be a murder, rapist, robbery, a racist, a con artist, if you admitted what you did was wrong, could see some repentance, a change of heart, even if happen a hundred, a thousand time. They might be racist toward Chinese, maybe a Black individual, didn't care what skin color, religion, economic background, if that person trying hard to do good in life, I won't mind extending grace by buying a cup of coffee, lunch, hell even some Chinese Food.

My comment to Abdul was "none of us are rich in Target, most of us are just getting by, the only rich person was Mitch, who happens to be store manager." I and he both agreed, either one of us wanted his position, because of the crazy hours he put in.

At times during the morning, normally joke around with Abdul, calling him "Bruce Lee number one son." His best friend Omar would be labeled as "Jackie Chan number son." The major obstacle, Omar, loved Bruce Lee too much, he carried too much pride with himself, could read his mind, always wanted to be called "Bruce Lee number one son, instead of Jackie Chan." Some day, when arrived early in the morning, I will say "ladies and gentlemen round number one, introducing "Bruce Lee Number One Son versus Jackie Chan Number One Son was being live at Target. Omar usual comment, "I am going to kick Number One Son Jackie Chan ass. Some wise guys will start laughing in the stockroom.

As time draw by, my minds drift away from Alice. By 10'0 clock in the morning, headed toward Human Resources to replace a battery on the gun, guessed who was sitting by one of the desk, none other than Sophie. She saw me coming in. "Hi, babe, hey Johnny is good to see you." I gave her a kiss on the cheek; she's very nice and happy. She wrote me a note, handled to me. It says "Johnny I am very proud of you. I notice that you are much happier and you have a good mental attitudes, keep it up, the Lord bless you. Sophie.

On my way to lunch this afternoon, I meet a very sweet woman, named Joanne, real nice lady. Every time I go there, always ended up with pleasant conversation, would start off simple stuff such as talking about the weather.

My first real countered with her was one day during my 3:30 noon break, brought some cookies, slipping some soda, noticed reading a book on "Ballet." I asked her "she's must be a ballerina." She replied "yes during those days was wonderful time, she's teaches dancing nowadays." I asked her if she ever heard of "Mikhail Gorbachev." "Johnny every ballerina in the world heard of his name." She said to be a ballerina and not know his name, must be horrible.

I commented Joanne "what do you think about those girls competing in synchronize swimming?" "Synchronize Swimming is a combination of ballet and gymnasium." She said. "They need to be physical strong as a weight lifter, move like a gymnast and be as graceful as a ballerina. We discussed a little about Esther Williams and her swimming movies. She told me "one a dancer reach middle age, about 40's they couldn't really danced any more, so most became instructor.

For some particular reason, I felt Joanne pain, trying her best to make ends meet for her only child, her daughter. She's had a crumply husband who's refused to pay child support. I clarified "never give up hope on God, he will provide for you." "Don't worry one day; you will receive child support from him. Her daughter was trying to apply for finical aid for college. To provide for her family, she also taught tap dancing at her parent dance studio. She clarified to me "her mother never gave her any credit in life; never acknowledge what she did in life." I said to her, "I really understand your life; my dad said angry words and indirectly putting me down, and though out his whole life gave me nothing, but low self-esteem. I loved getting pizza from her, out of the entire cook in Target, she made the best pizza, boy it taste delicious and the best chocolate cookies. I normally purchased the pepperoni. She usually tells me "to buy the pizza with chicken on it." That happens to be my favorite one also.

I shared with Joanne, "not only Blacks, Asians, other minorities are suffering, there a quick of few poor White folks desperately making head above water." I said "somehow the media and press are control mostly by liberal folks." "They are usually one-sided distorting the picture, they aren't giving the picture, when economic hardship arrived, and it bears no skin color across America, as the economy go back, especially nowadays when recession hit, the people most affected are the single mother with the weight on their shoulder.

Some day I found it hard to consecrate on my work. My mind kept flowing back to Kansas City to Clarisse. Clarisse was a pretty girl; she looks great, when she brailed her hair, meaning putting it in a bund. Nowadays not many girls French brailed their hair, back during the 1960 to 1980; it was a sexy thing for girl to show their famine side. Is very sad, almost hardly any women brailed now, they just let it hang loose.

My physical body was in New York, but my mental stage was still occupied in Kansas City. For some awe things, I couldn't shake off what went on in Kansas City, still haven't settled the issues became friends and people who hurt or disappointed me.

My main obstacle in life was not willingly to forget, to let go of the past. Some people like friend Richard in Boston told "me don't be too hard on yourself." "Johnny you can't help how you feel, most people don't know you have a very serve illness, is very easy for them to say stop struggling with your feeling and moved on with yourself, they don't understand, because they are not in your shoe." He said. "Johnny when you wake up in the morning, you don't choose how you're going to feel today, you need to know, how much you could handle in life, your limitability." He said.

Whenever I see cars, dirt, crowd, hear loud noises, wished I could returned back to Kansas City. I couldn't figure out, but I believed I saw some sign stating the population of Kansas Missouri was not even close to a million people.

"Hey Johnny five, how are you doing?" Alex said. "The Italian and the Chinese gangster go hand in hand." I said. "You're damn right about that." He said. "Hey Johnny how about paid day, you buy me some Chinese Food." He said. "Not right now I am a little broke." I said. "Sure you are, you're fifty lairs, and I know all you Chinese folks had lot monies in the Swiss Bank, a six-digit figure." He said.

One thing which determines me and Alex from the rest of the crowd that we were Queens's boys, being Queens Boys, we had something in common. We were tough and mean, didn't take any crap from any of you Long Island folks, we're street fighter, meaning fighting, when people weren't watching, if they turned their back on us, we're jump them from behind.

Another common virtue, we shared was food. Somehow many people liked Chinese and Italian cuisine. Pasta is what to Italian, as rice to Chinese. My favorite Italian dish was meatballs and spaghetti. Lasagnas, cold cuts, chickens with Avalos sauces, common joke was to marry a fat Italian woman, so you're be well fed.

One of the customers asked him "where certain things were?" Guess what his answer? "I am not clock in yet." I am just going to identify his ethnic, because wanted to protect his name. It turned out this fellow was a nasty, not a pleasant worker, very selfish individual.

He was a Black fellow that brail his hairs. I usually saw him in the break room. One day I and Alex friends called me "Johnny Five", for no particular reason, started laughing real loud. I was pretty angry with this wise character, didn't even knew me and he started to ridicule me.

Another circumstances I was putting some of the frozen meats away, one day, he approached me with something, I though he meant the price, but spoke to me I n a real nasty way "yon where does it belong." He asked. I said "give it to me, I'll put it away." I said. Afterward we stared at each other angrily.

I had no option, but to report him to Human Resources for ridiculing my name. The manager said "he will have a serious talk with him. A couple of days, later he spoke angry words to me, as I was leaving the HR office, turned around saw Jennifer and said "hi" to her, next thing, you know this person, walking right in front of me, I said "excuse me", because didn't wanted to bump into him, his responded was "what your problem." Boy this guy nasty attitude, how could he afford to hold a job?

My personal opinion if an individual have a negative attitude, similar to this individual. How do you expect anybody to hire you? Wise guys are the worst people in any employment, because they think, they know everything. I did know if he was from the city. Why come out to suburban middle class neighborhood and give clients or customer a hard time?

The following day, headed off to Human Resources as usual, Alice gave me a hard time. I requested "for a small gun, because I am in market." "Johnny we don't have a small gun, you used what we have, right now." She answered angrily. There were times I loved to file a complaint against her to HR. Unfortunately she had friends there. I guessed she treated all the L.O.D. and exec. Nice, so even if I filed a complaint, it won't go anywhere.

Her view was as long as she required doing her own work and nothing more than she has won't give you a hard time. She's give you a hard time, whenever you asked her to do something. I had some strong feeling, he had many issues against men, I don' think I ever saw her having harsh words with any of the women at Target.

As I was heading toward the back room stock, a very pretty Black girl named Kareem asked about me "hey Johnny are you all right, I am sorry, I heard you fell on the floor, the other day, so I though you went to the hospital, are you alright, fit to work?" "Oh wow thank very much that was very nice of you to think about me." I answered her.

"Johnny this job don't paid too much, you do the best you could, but please don't kill yourself, hurt or injury is very expensive to go to the hospital." She said. "Wow do you know is the same group of people, I didn't admire too much, yet Kareem out of her heart reach out to me." I said to myself.

God could be very strange person. It is always the people you hated the most were the one, either reaching out, making sure, you're o.k., caring for you. Jesus quoted in the bible "when there suffering, somehow there also compassion."

Some time on a Friday, when is paid day, I would go into the back room stock and said "listen everybody today is Friday, try to guess what that means is none other than paid day, and go have some Chinese Food. Most of the Blacks guys and Women will be laughing. Kareem would be laughing like crazy. One Black girl said to me "Johnny we just had Chinese Food yesterday." "Well today is pay day." I responded. Kareem would say "Johnny I heard you are very rich, your parent own Chinese restaurant, and you have a lot of monies in your account." "No you have it all wrong Kareem, I am not rich at all, when my parent first arrived in the United States, and English was not our first language, my dad worked 12 hours in the Chinese restaurant, my mom worked in the garment district." "We didn't have a whole lot to eat, unlike most middle class Americans, didn't own too much material stuff, beside if I am rich, I won't be working for Target." After what I mentioned to her, she's starting to crack up.

The following day, early dawn around 5:50a.m. I meet David Fool Man Chug at Queens Boulevard, waiting for my ride to Target, to my surprise his car was there, but he wasn't inside, so I looked around and noticed he was purchasing something from the street vendor.

"Hey Fool Man Chug good morning, "hey Johnny I am getting an egg sandwich on a roll." He said. "Do you like to have one?" "Sure why not, if you buying it."

It was mid-October, the wind happen to be raw, no longer gentle, and it was harsh, mid 40F. Summer was fading away, nice cool weather, nowhere in our sight. The message behind the autumn wind, no matter where the person was, either at school or work, this the time for trails to see if one could persevered in life. One might be in school, midterm time, being on the job needed to stand out among others.

The ride to Target happens to be very boring. We did not have too much to discuss about. He told me "if you wanted to return to Kansas City, you could, the major difficulty had to learn how to drive. "N.Y.C. has the best public transportation, no other place like her, so soon as you leave New York, to go any where else, you must obtain a driver license, or else you're trap in jail." He commented. "If you go back to Kansas City, stay away from John; don't go back to the International House of Prayer, because Clarisse will be still hanging out there.

He explained to me "running away is never the issues, what I had is inside of my heart, I carried an angry issue, no matter where I go, I am going to have that anger at other places, is not what inside, internal, not external. "You think your John Ho might look good external, because he possessed a beautiful wife, children's, nice house up on a hill, own two cars, he is blessed by the "American Dream", but don't let it fool you, like everybody else he has problems to solve, you might not see it.

He went on to share with me concerning an individual who left N.Y.C. to live in the Bahamas. In the Bahamas was a great resort paradise, some would labeled it as "Heaven on Earth." His next statement took me totally off guard, "you know what happen Johnny, next the man went out for a walk and he saw a person committed suicide, by hanging himself on a tree, just to say location is never the solution, if you ever wanted to return to Kansas City must deal with the anger in your heart, which is internally, not externally.

As I got to Target, Halloween was in the spirit of Target. Strange customs, hanging out on children department, a whole stack of candies arrived at the stock room. Putting out the candies wasn't that bad, we carried peanut butter, Reese, Hershey, chocolate, marsh mellow candies.

At this point, felt a little confident in answering some of the customer questions. I would tell them the E section, that where we had some of our Halloween snacks on sale. They were very happy to hear about that.

Putting those candies was pretty fun, similar to playing basketball, like tossing into the empty shelf. There's time, I made believe if I am doing a sky hook and dumped into the shelf, unfortunately some occasion, they fell on the floor.

There were people wearing difference colorful customs. Omar gave everybody a good laugh, by putting on a funny mask. When Toni was storing away the detergents, I pointed to Omar and she was laughing loudly. Some guys dressed up as Superman, while other as Batman and the Karate Kid.

Somehow wearing funny customs, made us felt like we one were once little kids, hopping off with our parents going to Trick O' Treat. I remember my first Trick O' Treat happen to be in Fourth Grade, those early days, kids carried the Ungifted box, a small empty carton for donation gather for poor children's in undeveloped nation. Receiving pennies was a pretty big thing in 1972, I even boosted how much pennies, and I got in my ungifted box
Halloween never did change that much, still American kid tradition. Is not just for little kids, even teenagers comes to people houses to collect candies and goodies. In every Halloween, no matter what age we are, there's still that little kid inside of our heart.

On Monday in the Human Resources Office, Phil the store owner announced "we have a new L.O.D. everybody; I want all of you to meet Jennifer." She seems very happy, cheerful and responded back nicely.

We just got the new gun in from our manufacturer. I needed to set in the control, since I am in the Market Department. I asked Phil and handled it to him, he didn't have any clue, and to my surprise Jennifer took my gun and tired her best to figure out the control. "Hi my name is Johnny." I said. "How will you like to be called Jens or Jennifer?" I asked. "Jens is fine." She responded. She was very pretty, had great figure, probably one of the prettiest girl in all of Target.

I knew right away, had established a wonderful working relationship with her. She carried the entire right characteristic of a lovely girl. If I wanted a girl friend she was the type I desired. She was sweet, kind, caring, helpful, and friendly toward all the employees.

Some co-workers bad mouthed Jens, admitting she was too pushy, when she wanted something she's demanded right away or go into the stock room. Some said "she wanted to present herself good in front of the other executive." ""Why she so nice to me I asked one of the employee? "Because you always help her", they said. I didn't pay too much attention by what they said. I go by how other people or how Jens treated me.

Well I guessed being charm by her beauty and feminine, my desired was to assist her. I recalled one occasion; I help her throw her garbage's. She was standing in front of about six garbage cans. She said "Johnny can you please help me throw the garbage's?" "Sure no problem" I said. After I dumped the garbage she even clapped her hand and said "yeah Johnny." Every time I saw her we're always smiled and shook hands with each other. There were times, I think about her and told some of the guys she was very pretty.

One girl asked me "why don't you ask Jens to join us for lunch sometime." I was deciding about it, then later on, I found out wasn't a good idea; you see she's an exec., so how the line must be drawn, in any working environment, don't mix business with pleasure. I don't believe in dating in any firm, while working. What you do, you must do it after work.

While I found out she was Jewish, even kept my distance more from her, because during the 80's, when I was in Queens College, had a Jewish girl who tutored me in English. She was very funny, sweet, friendly and nice. She's love to giggle, sat very close to me. I guess she's the perfect girl to ask out, so I did ask her. You know what her remark, "you're Chinese and I am Jewish, I only go out with Jewish guys." Wow I was so shocked to by her statement, entire body frozen, couldn't opened my mouth. When I told her "I had a girl just as friend." She kept on asking me "was she's Chinese." My friend David Fool Man Chug even said to me "well she's being honest to you." Is nothing wrong to be honest, but you can't said racist comment to the opposite sex, if they had an interest or desire to be your friend, that just totally, absolutely inexcusable. I don't care if they're trying to be honest with anybody. At the same time I was very glad, I knew Jens, the same way I knew Gina and was happy to assist in any way I could.

The old expression "is if you treated anybody nice, in return, you usually received the same thing. If you're friendly, kind, compassionate, helpful to other, friendly, greeting people, in return people would do the same. If an individual was cruel, evil, bad manner, easily angry, very few workers and managers like to be around those individuals.

I treated Jens nicely; in return she did the same. I didn't expect to date her or asked her out, I kept my distance. With a woman, sometime was very difficult. There were few who happen to be pretty. They looked good externally, but possessed rotten personalities. In any working environment very tempting, my solution if some women, very good looking, having a nice body, doesn't necessary meant you had to greet them, be nice or assist them, don't expect any favor in return, meaning lower your expectation on beautiful women or less you're be hurt 20 times more.

Not only women, these hold true for men also, if you performed something good, don't expect the same favor. Unfortunately we reside in a very selfish society. In America there's no such thing as a free lunch. Even in ancient period, favors were exchanged among each other. On the other hand, can't always be on the receiving end, in life, if received, must also learn how to give.

For a chance of pace, this afternoon, decided to take the Long Island Railroad. For the first time in my life, felt some kind of big shot, similar to those top executives working in the corporate office in Manhattan. Don't be surprise, very crowded also, most of the Blacks transferred at Jamaica station to take the Brooklyn line, while the other crowd headed down toward Penn Station in Manhattan.

The two good things about the train, I got home, two hours earlier, plus more leg room, much less crowded than the Nassau County N20 bus. Imaged myself in one of those war movie, where I kissed my girlfriend goodbye, threw her a banquet of flowers, imaging her quoting "Johnny write to me, everyday, please come home alive and I love you."

Terrance told me to come in a little before 7 a.m. if I didn't knew where everything was, told me to walk around to familiarize the departments. It was kind of funny, as I was walking and greeting everybody good morning, this time difference, decided to say "hi" to Blacks also. You known, almost everybody gave me a good response, just maybe one or two didn't.

I imaged myself in the airport, every department an airline, acted similar to a taxi driver, waving, chanting, and asking people "how are you doing today?"

One thing I like about Toni, I didn't cared if she came from the hood. Whenever I greeted, asked her "how she doing?" She normally gave me a polite response. You could said she was even better than any of the Chinese people in the mall, if she's pushing two tubs or carrying a heavy carton, I normally opened the door for her, she never refused to thank me.

Nowadays I asked myself, where the hell is everybody courtesies, good manner, maybe a lot of was how you were brought up by their parents or who the people they hung out with.

The other day, while I was riding the Long Island Railroad from Jamaica, going to Forest Hills there sitting behind me, this wise little boy no more than 8 or 7 years old was crying out "chi-chow, chi-chow Chinese. "Who the hell was saying these to me?" I whispered to myself. I turned around, noticed it happen to be a little boy, but I heard his mother whispering in his ear, "shish, shish there's a man sitting in front of us."

I turned around smiled, waved at the women, I couldn't remember. I think she smiled at me. My action to her was I gave you a lot of credit for disciplining your son, is o.k. he meant no harm, he doesn't know better, his only a little kid. If his mother decided to join in with him or didn't correct his words, then most people would be extremely upset. When their parents don't correct their children's and getting bad influence with peer pressure with the group of people they hung out with, at an early age most likely they became juvenile delinquent.

Every morning I saw Tom always working hard. I usually called him Tomas. I speak a little Spanish so Tomas mean Tom in Spanish. Another person I usually run into in the morning was Jason, often cracked a few jokes with him. You're one of the hardest working L.O.D. don't worry when I see those big shot, I am going to tell them to give you a rise." "Oh Johnny thanks you very much, you made sure you kept your promised." "You're like an engine in Target, none stop." I don't want to see being admitted to the hospital, because the bills are very expense." You're right, thank you very I'll remember that." He said.

When one of the overnight cleaning ladies stole my soda, I believed it was the same person that took my sandwich. Since one of the L.O.D. didn't do anything about it, Jason told me "that zero tolerance." When it comes to stealing other employees stuff, he sternly spoke to that particular woman and gave her a strict warning not to steal from any of the Target employees ever again or else she's be out of a job. There are three cheers for Jason.

I definitely agree with Jason, stealing from your co-workers was consider a very low, a kind of dishonesty, if somebody willingly to tell the truth, must revealed, not just words, but we as workers needed to back up our action. It wasn't long one of the team leader was let go, because he violated Target policy by giving his employee discount to his relative, but this woman, I truly suspected was not only stealing my drinks and food, but also other co-workers personal items, still able to hold on to her job.
Andy from electronic gave me a ride home this afternoon. He told me "where I live." I told him "around the Queens Center Mall on Queens Blvd. He started the same hours and ended the same hours, so it worked out perfectly. He said "he's heading toward that direction also." I offered to give him a couple of bucks for the gas monies or buy him a soda, he kept on refusing.

As I was riding in his expensive sport car, struck an interesting conversation, like striking oil. Conversation turned to a gold mine.

I and he had something in common and that was music. He asked me "what type of music I enjoyed?" I answered "music before your time meaning the sixes which consisted of the "Beatles", "Rolling Stone", "Bee Gees", "Peter, Paul and Mary." Then the 80's with "Air Supply, "Phil Collins", "Journey", Jefferson Starship", finally the 90's with "Richard Max", and "Bryan Adams."

I didn't admire the Rap nowadays they called "Hip Hop, told him, most of it is violent and racist. I said "after "Richard Max" and "Bryan Adams", the music was sucks." I think he agreed with me.

I explained to him "music in the sixes was a message for Civil Rights, Anti-War, bad things, which I am not crazy, happen to be drugs. We think songs, lyrics made a person feel happy, and life was too stressful nowadays, with everybody trying to get ahead in life. Music could also be a form of physical or mental health. It takes the mind of wordiness.

He asked me "if I had any hobbies?" I mentioned "writing and cooking." He questioned me "what kind of food I like to cook?" I answered "Chinese, Italian and American Cuisine." He also Chinese like most workers at Target. He mentioned "Chinese Food, the hardest to cook." I disagreed and said "French Cuisine the toughest, because most of it, consisted of heavy cream, mixed with milk and butter.

Luis from Green World, the one who Sam sends him to help me was a great guy. It happen to be my distance niece birthday today, I believed she's three or four years old. I requested him, if his sister who worked in the Bakery would bake a cake for my niece. He answered "no problem." I said "the cake for four or five people.

I explained to him, I once employed in the bakery, while in a summer camp, up in Canada, I learned to bake bread. Baking bread wasn't too difficult. The only hard part was the yeast. You needed to use lukewarm water; it the liquid, considered too hot or cold, it would destroy the yeast.

I let him knew baking was a very fun, unique, rewarding occupation, contrast to laboring at Target. Jobs at Target was very boring, most of the work, me and Luis putting away stuff on the shelf. He clarified to me "ringing up the merchandises to the customers, they're fight for their last dollars, quartets, nickels, dimes and even pennies.

I persuaded to him when it came to Baking, there's a form of creativities, talents involved. The design and decoration signaled certain pride for you, performing any form of culinary arts consider a master skill, could be passed down to cross generation.

I and Terrace waged an all out ugly war with each other. I was trying to kiss his ass, by being nice to him, staying late, sometime on a Friday night, cleaning yoga spilled, the day I vomited had a high fever early in the morning, still reported to work. I though he was going to give me a break.

Then one day I appeared to work, "Johnny I am going to put you on the candies." "What do you mean, just said that to me one more time." I was mad as hell, burning sulfur like a hot volcano ready to erupt. "I worked just as hard as anybody else, this is not fair, other employees from our department took long lunch and 15 minutes break, even taken days off, just what the hell, you had to say to them.".

He complained I was too slow, not fast enough. To be in Market you had to pull away the frozen goods quickly or else it gets containment and people could tell is stink, then the L.O.D. will get on your case.

"Yeah when your friends or bubby goof off you don't disciplined them refused to take any action, you just worried about covering your own ass, like the other L.O.D. tried to make yourself looked good in front of your superior, you're don't give a damn about us, you're very selfish.

I was so shocked, there wasn't any retaliation from him, even said "hi" to me in the morning, smiled at me and asked me "how I was doing?" I expected some kind of shouting match with him. I carried a full load of ammunitions, which consisted of evil, cruel and nasty, even ready to give him the index finger, said the F or SH word.

I was crying to myself "help me, somebody, anybody in Target, Bob Margaret, Justin, Peter Son, Big Sean, Little Sean, Frank, Chris, Andy, the two Luis, Ron, Ron from HR, John the China man, even Alice who I labeled as grand mom, Finny, Mitch and finally Jens, if any of you had any cold water, please poured it on me, I am burning like a wild Forest fire, please you guys needed to cool down my burning anger.

I learned the fact of life, in any working environment, is nothing wrong to as or assist your supervisor or co-workers, on the other hand, don't expect you're get favorable treatment some supervisor will not return the same favor. If the individuals saw me kissing every manager butt, they're said "this guy Johnny he just wanted to make himself looked good in front of the L.O.D."

The rule of the thumb, you do the best you could with any employer, firm, nothing wrong in offering your service. The Department of Labor in the United States, took a survey. The main question was job scarification, guessed what the answer was, not monies, not so much on promotion, but assisting other employees and customers.

For example when our yoga was on sale, many times, they went out quickly, first I told them, and delivery came on Mondays, Wednesdays, and Fridays. Often I would go to the back freezer to search for particular yoga bran name. I climbed over the skid and gave it to the customer, at times; they asked me "if we had any cereals bran inside the stock room." If I found any, when I handed to them, I saw a big smile on their face or gave them a ring check, seeing a smile on their face; really made my days feel much better.

Another whom I usually had good conversation was Donald. I used to work for Grumman Aerospace aviation. We discussed during the Second World War, Grumman manufactured the F4F Wild Cat, and in the beginning was not match for the Japanese Zero fighter. The early days of the war, at the battle of Midway the Wild Cat defended her by flying in pair, knows as wing man tactic, which was still used today by Top Gun instructor. Later on in 1943 Grumman created the F6F Hellcat, when it first came out, the Zero no longer ruled the sky.

Donald boosted, took great pride working for this organization. I don't blame him one bit. I am pretty sure most of us saw the movie "Top Gun" casting Tom Cruise, the F-14 Tom Cat was made by Grumman aviation aerospace firm. The F-14 was equipped with a pilot and co-pilot during the Iraq war in "Operation Desert Strom." It proved its accuracy. It carried short range heat-seeking deadly SideWinder missile and radar quipped Sparrow missiles.

Every time I saw him, we talked about dog fighting seem to be the most interest. We admired the P-40 War Hawk, stationed in China was refer to as the "Flying Tiger." The key element in Donald pointed "out in tackling the Zero, always dived on it." "You couldn't dive in front of it, then the enemy would be on your tail, so had to dive at the enemy aircraft at a certain angle." This was a hit and run tacit developed by a man named Claire Chennai.

Both I and he agreed in any dog fighting was a pilot war, maneuverability's, quickness, speed, sharp reflexes, if a pilot obtain all those qualities, then you refer him as the elite, maybe being called "Top Gun."

Somehow being in Target, we could all picture ourselves as either fighter bomber or transport pilot. Imaged the tube, loaded with items to be put on displayed would be the transport pilot. The bomber pilot could be the sale person, locating a customer, persuading him or her to create a sale. Fighter pilot would be the last line of service knows as the cashier, when they ringed up the price. If a cashier ringed up five clients, then he or she had 5 kills and was considered an ace.

November was here, that meant Thanksgiving was around the corner. New faces were pouring in the store. They were like solider gearing to go into combat. It felt like, we were preparing for the big invasion. It meant there was going to be more overtime pretty soon.

Strange as it may seem, when I was at high school and college, couldn't waited until Thanksgiving was here, because by October midterm season was over. After Thanksgiving was over, Friday happened to be the big shopping day. At night we usually had a big Thanksgiving dinner at my church.

After the big feast we all shared what we needed to be thankful toward God. Some would thank God for these and that. To me as a believer, we should always be thankful not just on this holiday, but everyday. Jesus said "is always blessed to give than to receive." I do admit when I gave, expect sometime, and a little in return, sometime even their friendship. On this thanksgiving, I thank God for provided me such wonderful and blessed co-workers, managers and friends for me.

Joanne was talking to me, the other day; her daughter was ill with a fever and happens to be her birthday. On my break, decided to purchase a c.d. for her daughter as a birthday present. It was a 1967 songs c.d. I pointed out some of her lyrics such as "Windy", Daydream Believer", "To Sir with Love", and "Both side now", was our time.

My first taste of giving without expecting anything in return, was when my friend Bobby gave me a laptop computer. Joanne told me "she couldn't afford to purchase a computer for her daughter, so I told her I am going to give my old one to her daughter." She was so thrill.

I never forget that day when David Fool Man Chug helped me delivered the computer to Joanne. She was so full of joy and happiness, to my surprise even her daughter, showed up at Target. As I was leaving that day, she said "Johnny my daughter is here, she wanted to thank you, and she wanted to write a thank you note to you." "Joanne that quite o.k. is not necessary, as long as she thank me in her heart, that the most importance thing, beside I am already late a couple of minutes in catching my train." I said. She introduced me to her and I was very happy.

That day there was an electrify feeling, I possessed in my heart, for the very first time, I done something good for an individual and didn't even expected a thank you note and she's happen to be very pretty.

I do admit when men do some thing good or kindness out of their heart for a pretty girl, they expect something in return from them, usually a date, having dinner in exchange for sexual pleasure. If the woman feel embarrassed, uncomfortable, that perfectly understandable, you know they had to protect themselves from aggressive men who tried to take advantage of them.

I had the opportunity to meet a real nice L.O.D. In his very word happen to be a real gentleman in the way he conducted himself. Just because his executive, he wasn't arrogant, demanding, boastful, or pride. In every action, speech, physical gesture, consider to be a gentleman in action, gentleman perfection. His name was George.

We introduced to each other one November morning. I joked about him "all you L.O.D. are very wealthy people, including yourself." "You probably have a six-digit figure money market account." "No Johnny I am just like you everybody else in Target making ends meat." He said.

The other day, he approached me and asked me something in regard to my department. I told him "the procedures, that our delivery comes on Mondays, Wednesdays, and Fridays, told him Fridays was our busiest day, most of the time on that average about 4 to 5 skid." I showed him, where our candies and grocery department was, the freezer, the frozen goods, where the milk, diary products, meats, eggs, cheese and yoga was located.

Afterward I said "I am sorry, I haven't really assisted you enough." "Oh Johnny don't worry about it, you had already done a whole lot for me." "What you showed me the operation of the department, where everything was located, the time and date of the delivery, that was a more than enough, next time, the good thing was what you taught me, and I could do the same for a new employee." Wow I said to myself, "this person, truly a born-again Christian, a believer not only in words, but through his good nature, he back it up in action.

As I was leaving work, that day to catch my train, I said "George you're a very nice person, hope to see you again, hopefully in this store." "Johnny whatever the good Lord had in store for me, I put my trust everything was under God hand, why don't we waited upon the Lord." He said. I said goodbye to him, I believed that was the last time, we saw, spoken to each other. Those few days, plus moments with George happen to be a great feeling. On those days "alone came a gentleman."

The following day, quietly announced to Ron over at HR, next week will be my final days at Target. I explained to him "during the Christmas season, especially the day after thanksgiving was going to be crazy, like a mad house. He mentioned to me "was totally understandable, I think you made a wise decision, I am not upset or disappointed in you at all." "I am proud and very happy, Johnny, you had made tremendous process, very happy for you, if you ever need a recommendation, or if you needed to return in the summer, to earn some extra monies, I am more than happy to assist you," He said.

I woke up around 4 a.m. this morning prayed for an hour, read a little bit of the bible, had my usual breakfast, a piece of cheese cake and a cup of coffee, took a shower, wore my Target uniform, wrote some letters to some employees, plus managers, wrapped some gifts for special friends of mine.

In my mind, those words kept echoing in my head. "Johnny today was your last day at Target. "No matter how upset your with the Blacks, if they're mistreated you, please don't seek for revenge, just simply let it go." "You started out at the right foot and you wanted toe end at the correct foot, because in the future if you ever needed to return or ask a favor from Human Resources from one of the manager, you needed to end in good terms.

I arrived at Queens Blvd. around 5:45 a.m. my usual time to wait for David Fool Man Chug. Just like old time, he brought me an egg sandwich for breakfast. During our ride, we spoke about my experiences at Target, the good times, bad, disappointing, angry moments, wonderful things that happen to me. He knew for me being in Target was great working experiences. In his mind he foreshadowed my working experiences would be the key to unlock the future for me. "I am very proud of you Johnny, I think you did a wonderful job, the way you conducted yourself; give yourself a big pat on the shoulder." He said. "What are you going to do next?" He asked. "I don't really know, maybe take it easy for a while, relax, and spend the time with my family with nieces and nephews."

"You enjoy writing, done you?" "Of course you know when it comes to writing, it is one thing I treasure, will never give it up, it is embattled in my blood, I consider it my pride and joy." "How about writing your experiences at Target, I am pretty sure, everybody will love to read it." "I don't need to tell you this, you know my weakness." "No I don't please tell me." "My English grammar is terrible, my typing very awfully slow, beside, needed somebody to edit my work." "Don't worry, you have a great imagination, if the publisher thinks your can sell, they're provide you with an editor."

Before my final day, I made up with Terrace, he was a great guy. To my acknowledge he, never told Ron I was a very slow worker, never went to HR to report me, never stabbed me from behind. I had too high of expectation on him. He was like me and you, working hard at a dead end job, trying to make something better for himself, which I don't, blamed anybody for that. I didn't told him I was leaving, the day before my final day at Target, very glad he accepted my apology, I got to see him face to face, talked like real man, most importance shook his hand.

One person I didn't wanted to leave out was Ron in charge of receiving. I haven't spent too much time with him; on the contrary every occasion with him was very pleasant. He never once criticized about my work performance or action. As a matter of fact, I even taught him some curse words in Chinese. The day I taught him, he was laughing out of his head. He knew I happen to be a hard working individual, sometime I guessed he saw me sleeping at the break room for more than 20 minutes. He never once approached me and said "Johnny why are you goofing off." He was extremely flexible with me, when I needed the weekend off, gave it to me. When I needed one day off to go to the social security administration, more than happy to he said "yes that perfectly o.k."

During his birthday I brought a Chicago c.d. for him, I said a funny thing "is o.k. Ron I am not going to ask you how old you are, in my book I still define you as a young duce." He said "he's 43 years old." I said "I am 46." "You don't look 43; look more in your early or mid thirties." "Oh thank you very much, Johnny, I'll remember that."

I might never see Ron again in the future, but I always wanted to shake his hand, mentioned those two words of thank you for giving me the opportunity to work in the market department and I think he will be very happy to hear that.

As usual my last day, I greeted everybody, took a glanced at the store, those few minutes held fond memories, remained me when I first came in, applied on the computer, going into Human Resources, doing zoning, working with Bob in the back stock room, putting away frozen foods in its location and assisting many clients. In my mind I felt sad of leaving, they said the Target at Hicksville, consider one of the best stores in New York, and you had people coming as far as Brooklyn to work here.

As I was strolling each department such as the electronic, I remember Luis, Andy, Finny and Marvin. In Blue world, there were Gina, Alex, in the cashier, they were Donald and Sophie. In Starbuck it was Anna, Mark, Pizza, Joanne, some of the very nice women, the shoe department, a very nice Latino girl every time I said "hi" to her, that's always a wonderful smile on her face.

I went to the back stock room, made sure, I got a chance to say goodbye to Kareem. She was a beautiful girl. I felt hard breaking the news to her. I told her "today to be my final day and since is going to be a busy day, I can't have a cup of coffee with you, I am going to give you three dollars to buy a cup of coffee." She refused; I kept on insisting, since I might be going back to school, she told me "to save my monies." I was so happy she finally accepted. "Make sure when you leave, come over and say goodbye to me." I said.

The big truck rolled in, our delivery came around 7 a.m. John dropped by around 10 minutes later, very glad to see him. How was

I going to break the news to him, I knew we needed all the help we could muster, Christmas only a month away. It wasn't easy, hate to leave John all alone. I learned the rope, the in, out, the dos and don'ts all the thing concerning the Market Department from him. I decided to break the sad news to him during our lunch session, because I didn't want to take a chance that he tells everybody.

It was so busy pulling in the skid with John, I had all forgotten about Kareem, around 10 a.m. headed toward Human Resources to get my gun, to my surprise she saw me. "Thank you very much Johnny, you're a kind, very nice person, is been good, I had a great time in knowing you, good luck to you whatever you do, I wish you the best of luck. I'll never forget you." With those compassion words, she kissed my forehead and we said goodbye to one another.

My final days working beside John was the greatest experiences in Target, as usual we talked crazy jokes, conversation often center around women, for him, he admired those Chinese girls, to be him consider them as gold, diamonds, the crown jewel, while I admired the Caucasian girl.

First order of the day, we usually store away the frozen stuff such as ice-cream, pizza, frozen chicken, Chinese cuisine and vegetables. It was great to have some extra help from temporary workers. Things were moving at a great pace.

I did almost run into a small incident with one of the Black woman. I needed to use the restroom she' standing there with her shopping cart. When I said "excuse me", she didn't want to move, then one of the Latino girls extremely nice. "We need to move our carts, so Johnny could go to the rest room." She said. "Thank you very much." I said. As I tired to open the door, it was locked. Then the woman said real cruel, evil, nasty words "see somebody cursed." I was mad as hell, simply no need for such outrageous comment, boy she really triggered my anger.

I was thinking of saying "you better watch what you said, wasn't very nice at all, no need for that." I decided to sallow my pride, walk away, while nobody was watching, close my eyes, said a silent prayer "God I am very upset, let me not seek out revenge, please help me to control my emotion and God, just let me forgive that woman, since this is my last day, let me not do anything to jeopardized myself, let me leave Target in good terms.

I finally gave the news to John; no he wasn't upset or disappointed in me at all. I took him for lunch, sharing our final meal, he called it the "The last Supper", of course he said the F word and some racist remarks to me, but I could care less, his way of saying farewell to me.

By 3 p.m., decided to go over to HR to say thank you to Ronald and wished to shake his hand, but the receptionist said he was in a meeting. I didn't wished to tell her is very final day, because I didn't wanted some of the employee to over hear what I said, so I gave the gift for her to put it in Ronald Mail box.

I also brought some present for other members but didn't wish to hand it to the receptionist. I desired to give those present secretly, didn't desired to create a big scene. "Wow this is great, how I am going to achieve this quietly." I said to myself.

All of a sudden I bumped into Bob, I let him today was my last day working in Target. I could tell right away, he felt sad. I figured deep down in his heart, knew I was a hard, good worker, the first time I work with him. We had great respect with one another. "Boy I am going to miss you Johnny, you been a great help, a great person, really hate to see you leave, wished you the best of luck. I told him, had a small gift for him, please come outside and we chanted just like time for those precious minutes.

Since me and him were a great Mets fan, I offered the 1986 World Champion New York Mets book. I knew he happen to be a big

N.Y. Islander Hockey fan, so I apologize, couldn't find any book on them. He said "that absolutely fine, really loved t he Mets, thank you very much Johnny."

Next thing, he asked me "What was my future." I told him, "wasn't sure, thinking of going into aviation maintenance to fix aircraft and tired my best to obtain the FAA and power plant license. He thinks is a very good trade, excellent field to go into.

I and Bob held a great chemistry, function very well as a team, and hate to see it come to an end. I'll always say he was the first team leader to look out for me.

He asked me "what can I do for you Johnny." I told me "if I ever needed to come back during the summer, could you speak to Ronald, if I could work for you in the back stock room?" I asked him. "You got yourself a deal, Johnny I'll make sure it happens." He responded. We hugged each other and said goodbye.

I stood outside, chanted for a few minutes with John. He gave me a sounded word of advice, "don't tell people your slow or have a learning disability, Target been very gracious and understanding in meeting your needs, not all companies, even supervisors, upper management would bend their back to accommodate you."

We reside in a very selfish world, you don't like it, and I don't like it either, but that reality, unfortunately every person is for themselves, but I know you have good heart, you do tired your best to assist other. We hugged each other, bid farewell with one another, as I walked away from him, I waved my hand and we smiled, the same expression, when he first introduced himself to me.

If was a short distance walk to the L.I.R. train station, I pictured every step I took to the station, tell a story of my work experiences at Target. "So this is Broadway Mall, its been great knowing this area, thank you for people and strangers whoever assisted me, even in the smallest way as possible, it meant a lot to me.

I purchased my ticket from the station, mentioned to the worker "you won't see me any longer, today my final day at Target." "Is ashamed you're a friendly, nice, great person, wished you the best of luck." He said. I told him is Friday, go enjoy your weekend and have some Chinese Food." "Oh I always have Chinese Food on Friday with my family." He said.

I stood at the platform silently, my mind was blank, and then I heard the announcer said "track1 and 2, 3:45 p.m. train to New York Penn Station, Woodside, Queens, and Forest Hill arriving on time." The choc, choc, train coming to pick me up. Once again I was going home for good. "All aboard please step in everybody." The conducted said. As the train traveling away from Hicksville station, my life at Target, gradually fading away, as it arrived at Jamaica station, final chapter of Target came to an end.

I got off at Jamaica Station. As I was standing there waiting at the platform for the Forest Hill train. I said "God is hard to say goodbye to all those lovely, warm, nice people, I am leaving behind. They weren't just ordinary folks. We had common values, ideas, and a boned chemistry on how to assist customer, made Target Hicksville one of the better place for employees to work and customer to shop. We weren't always perfect, but we never stop trying, we never gave up, indeed we weren't superman, if didn't satisfy our employees or customer, we corrected ourselves.

As I stood there, could help myself. There was a little tear in my eyes. They said in the Chinese culture crying is a form of weakness. As a little boy, I cried a lot, my sisters, brother and parent scolded at me. I assumed in Western American and Asian culture, we don't really show our emotion too much. I couldn't care less what other people said how they got the nerve to say men are not suppose to cry, only women. On this day, couldn't hold back those tears. Those fire months, I learned about myself as a person, got the taste of what is reality all about.

I left Target quietly, because didn't want any big celebration, didn't wish to create a scene. I think in my heart I done the right thing by keeping myself a low profile.

I endured, persevered, survived to leave Target in good term, each day; I struggled to keep myself out of trouble that was my true victory. On this day, I could proudly proclaimed "Farewell to Target Hicksville."

Footnotes

1
    Leon Uris Exodus
(Bantam Books: New York, 1958) pp. 4

Bibliography

Leon Uris. Exodus. New York, 1958

FLOWER FOR SHARON

Oh Sharon sweetest, dearest, love undivided, merciful, towering
over heaven, shower of flowering falling on your grave.

Wealth and fame I do not have.

Whisper a song in your memories.

That day you were taken away, our nation weeps your pain.

Oh mighty God we cried, why her life ended so short.

The day you were born, came a precious, priceless
commodity, which cannot be replace.

Eyes flashing as emerald stone, hair shining heart of Gold.

A figure with vinegar, jigger men emotion.

For those who known you were more
beautiful inside than outside.

A heart radiant, flamboyant, desiring
to seek, for the less fortunate.

The fateful day of August 1969, we felt
rage and demanded justice.

The day you perish, Hollywood was never
the same, vanished with your name.

Oh Sharon today we looked upon the sky, you smiled upon us.

Oh Sharon may you rest peacefully, gently,
happiness flooded your heart.

Tonight, tonight we see your love.

Tonight angles with flaming torches
keep a virgin watch over you.

Lyrics taken from Beatles "Lucky in the Sky with Diamond."

This is a story about Sharon Tae who was killed by members of the
Charles Mason Family around August 1969.

FOOD SERVED ON HER DELIGHT

If Cuisine happened to be international
delight will cherished every minutes.

Smorgasbord for Norwegian, Fried Rice for Chinese
meatballs for Italian people wasted foods no success.

Delight a great cook for the hungry.

Hungry individuals, meal for your soul.

Wanton Soup, Clam Chowder served on a bowl.

A steak dinner rhymed with shrimp Loin Mei.

I guessed most women and men now tried to be slim.

Hamburger with fires over a milk shake.

For Thanksgiving plenty of turkey to be bake.

Delight heart go out for the starving.

Underneath her a loved of caring.

Apple Pie, Cherry Pie, Blue Berry Pie, presented on a sliver.

Vanilla Cake, Chocolate, Cake, ice-cream greatest desert.

Her loved for hungry people will be exerted.

Chinese over Norwegian, Irish desired American Cuisine,
French desert with heavy cream overflowed on

Delight greatness.

GENTLEMAN PERFECTION

Gentleman greatness melts in his heart.

Wonderful friendship spindled us apart.

Adorabling embracing your holy flame.

Kindness, sweetness, compassion kindle in Steve name.

Turned back clock let imagination guide like a wind.

Knew my expression flowed in the sky as mankind.

If I had the time would buy this world for you.

Jesus loving words come unto me, heavy laden, give me your ore.

In this selfish world, you gave your heart to me.

If could paid you back, our savior was born in Bethlehem.

Go ahead people filled your mind with anger.

Steve endless love covered it with a hanger.

Steve love, equality for a better world is
beyond our understanding.`

Knowing human suffering spelled like a ring.

In June of 1984 imaginary and poetic departed.

One day Jesus miracle in all mankind would integrate.

Could never give you this world; write
until tear dropped from my face.

Time after time Steve and Johnny writing
would leap to outer space.

Steve your humble majesty Jesus Christ writes a
song in your heart, as your personalities

Fly like a kite, for this day you are gentleman perfection.

Sincerely, Johnny Wong

'98 5 23

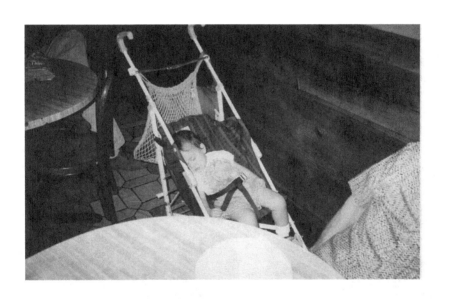

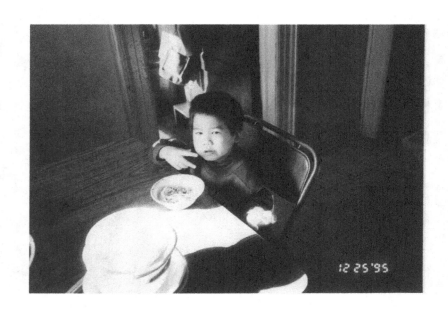
12 25 '95

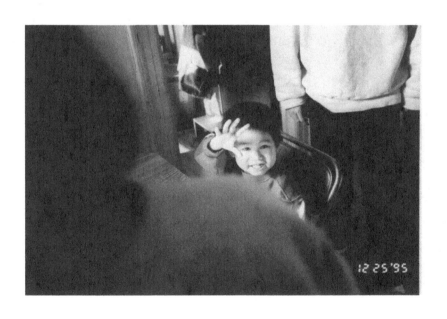

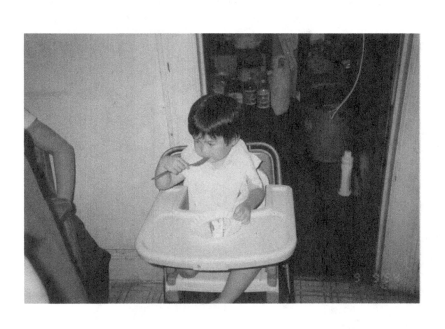

GIRLS, GIRLS

Lying in my bed, the clock ticking on a Saturday morning, as the needle struck 8 0' clock daydreaming begin, waking up, dawn of a new day. Unlike other universe, my world was full of excitements, funs, magics and surprises. I normally dream of girls.

They come from all colors, Blacks, Whites, Asians, Spanish and Indians, all sizes, heavy, skinny, tall, short, averages, come from all places.

Northern girls, composed of Italians, Jewish, and Chinese. Most of them settled in New York usually have long Brown hairs. Scottish and Irish girls are from the Mid West. Germans girls their origin Pennsylvania, consisted of long blonde hair with blue eyes. California girls are wild and crazy.

GOD KNOWS HOW LONG

Some said lived by feeling.

Can we trust them?

Memories of past bring hurting.

God knows how long our pain.

Our life seems emptiness.

Each day we struggle.

Tears drops bring sadness.

Each day we endurances

We lived by dream.

Life takes a chance.

Some dream worth a scram.

Good times we danced.

Problems never seem ending.

Some times wished could be vanishing.

Be great if gone with wind.

We are difference born with disease.

Wealth and fame not the solution.

Situation holds separate piece.

Lack of understanding, add complication.

Someday, somewhere, a new era.

Leave yesterday behind.

For tomorrow will refine.

For Tomorrow a day away

By Johnny Wong

GREATEST GUY IN C.T.

Stan is the man.

Name of the game is to love Jesus.

Emotion and compassion flow in his heart.

Commission, mission blew Stan to obey.

His expression for Jesus loves the greatest.

Confession shove him the greatest.

Stan strife after Jesus heart.

His life copy Jesus chart.

Stan action speaks louder than words.

Comfort other in love, never in anger.

Explain other in love always express kinder.

On Chinese New Year he turned into a smoking dragon.

On American holiday chewing on hot dogs and apple pies.

Before I left for I hop knew God performance miracle in my life.

Returning home God electroform Johnny life.

On this Christmas day greatest guy to ever walk
among Christian Testimony Church.

Sincerely

Johnny

HARD OF GOLD

Lisa heart unfolds like heaven, calling on a landslide.

She clothed splendid majesty towing fountain seaside.

Angel wrapped in golden amour.

Her sweet life flashes in drama.

On that day my anger was burning with no relief.

Sweet beautiful angel sent from heaven with belief.

Wonderful compassion words took away pain.

Sky opened shower of blessing felt like rain.

Johnny can purchase the world for me
will never get wrong impression.

One day wonderful statement made a lasting expression.

Powerful prayer foreshadowed my future.

Returning home my life will be a fortunate.

Told her to get out didn't want to cry.

She said Jesus honor you if could see your eyes.

Lisa eyes with fire, melting like honey, sweet
as the honey comb, heart hard of Gold.

Sincerely,

Johnny Wong

HEAVENLY ANGEL

Joanne heavenly angel sent forth.

Speaking words of widow.

Comforting others pains.

Clothed in righteousness.

Every tears melt in her heart.

Living in Christ love.

Understanding human suffering.

Can never hurt a fie.

Soft as the gentle breeze.

Actions louder than words.

Loves people with all her heart.

Seeing her never a dull moment.

Tears flows with compassion.

Words can never describe how beautiful you are.

A moment in birth is a moment with Joanne.

How can Jesus fall for you?

No greater love than to be you.

Story goes round and round.

No greater joy than to be with Joanne.

Sincerely

Johnny

HIS GREATEST GIFT

His greatest gift is a piano.

Magic spread from his hand.

Every note, he strikes tells a story.

A note name is Alan Rathe.

B notes the song he brings.

C notes Christ center perfect match.

E notes lyrics sings.

F notes friendship hatch.

G notes gratitude in wings.

C major center on Elissa greatness.

F major is Christ faith in action.

G major his glory lyrics is desire.

E major is Elissa gorgeous bride.

B major his brilliant dazzled in fantasy.

A major almighty confined in encore.

Half step Alan reaching to others.

Whole step is expressing folklore.

Ebony is exceeding together.

Ivory is exceeding God world.

Flats and sharp voice echo.

Scales and chord dance to beat.

Intervals and octaves dance to disco.

By Johnny Wong

IHOP GIRLS

The I hop girls march all around, all around singing
praising Jesus Christ from morning tonight.

They pray over Johnny insomnia told him Jesus sing a loveable.

Debbie prophecies I am the Moses baby flowing on the Nile.

I said hello to them they gave me a friendly smile.

They cracked up at my New Yorker Chinese Boston accent.

I told them my nieces and nephew is half Irish.

They gave a pleasant smile, said what lovely family you have.

The funny Texas woman said I talk like a little Chinese duce.

Every time I asked for a cup of coffee she started to laugh.

She loves those New York accent, it cheers her day up.

The I hop girls always thank me when I pray for them.

They looked at me, wonder what hell he's writing about.

Could he be writing about I hop crazy's girls.

All the girls go to sleep, he is still writing away.

Is it true one day Johnny diary going to get published?

Will we be famous or starving for Chinese food?

They told me if I afforded a million buck
they won't live in New York.

One day I packed my bag and went home.

As I returned home they all forgotten about Johnny.

Is sad to say that how the story ends.

IMAGINARY AND POETIC

Someday out of the sky.

Imaginary and poetic collide.

In a world falling apart.

In a word of suffering.

We speak of a story of endless love.

Not long ago a paradise in Eden.

Maybe we can fellowship in love.

God knows how long.

We can bring this place together.

In place worth a thousand people.

Imaginary and poetic tells a story.

A story beyond our compassion.

A tale conquers all evil.

As soon as our heart speaks a melody.

We will be resting in God anthem.

Imaginary and poetic sing a lyric

Yesterday and today, we endure.

For tomorrow a day away.

We will wake up the drawn of new day.

A day, we live in peace.

In heaven many rooms prepare for us.

Sincerely, Johnny Wong

IN EVERY WORLD THERE A CHILD IN US

In every child, a cried of innocent, a cried of yesterday, tomorrow, a cried for a better world.

In Julie world little kid learned to speak, played, walked and grows to their potential. Some leaned the alphabet, while other excelled the area of science and math. Little boy dressed up as cowboy, they played with sword imaged themselves in shining armor, while little girl put on beautiful custom and danced as graceful ballerina.

My session with Julie a moment in time is also a moment in birth. The day our daddy and mommy carried us home from the hospital, our precious journey began. No said life was fair and easy. None of us were wealthy; we do the best with what we have.

In our session we emphasized the importance of family, religion, duty, country, citizen. Julie taught me to think of those who are less fortunate, to reach out to them.

In Julie world little children will have enough to eat, clothe to wear, toys to play, a decent place to live.

In her world every child cried for a better world.

From

Johnny

JERSEY BOY AND NEW YORKER BOY

If there were a time Jersey Boy and New
Yorker Boy are arch rivalries.

Drew would be charging across the Hudson with his cavalry's.

New Yorker Boy and Jersey Boy are
separated by the mightily Hudson.

On a clear day could see swarm of people
marching across the river liked Vulcan.

People from both side hurried to meet the American dream.

Consuming to get ahead, they hurtled together as a team.

Both New Yorker and New Jersey had
some thing in common the bar.

When finishing drinking on a clear night, sky light up with star.

Drew, John the Baptist loves to crown in
bar to witness to pretty women.

All the pretty women begged him to write a poem.

Jersey Boy and New Yorker boy separated by a river apart,
inherited common valves, and principles, lived side by
side, worked side by side, consumed greed side by side.

By

Johnny Wong

JOANNE, JOANNE, HEAVENLY ANGEL

Joanne, Joanne, heavenly angel Jesus adored.

Jesus your darling savior.

Loving others is her commodore.

She turns hated into affection.

Listen to her loving heart.

Let us not be in anger for our collection.

Put on a smiled, she will give a tart.

Her sweetness, charmed a reflection.

Take your burden she's stored in part.

For life is very short, needed confession.

Lead on Joanne, she's teaches us motherhood.

Joanne, Joanne, how lovely is your strength.

Carrie Anne, Mary Anne, Joanne, be your parenthood.

Can't go on living, Joanne will carried your weight.

JOHN F. KENNEDY

The year was 1960. We enjoyed wealth and luxury. Jobs were plentiful, babies begin born, people brought and sold. We were a young nation with dreams ahead of us. A young man in office, named John F. Kennedy.

When he spoke, electrified a whole crowd challenged our youth to be the leader of the world. "Ask not what your country can do for you; instead ask what you can do for your country." He said.

His handsome looks, wealth and pretty wife charmed our nation. He ruled our nation like an Iron Fist, everything he did was most likely to succeed.

He spoke out against injustice of the world, speech similar to a weapon to fight against evilness. Then in 1961, declared the New Frontier Program. In foreign policy, stood firm, won't comprised with any countries.

Then on that fateful day of 1963, disappeared from us, no longer hear or see you, was killed by an assassin bullets. The whole world stood, watch, weep and mourn for our beloved president, not only we lost a president, but a world leader, no longer hear your speech, see your smile, shake your hand, watch you on T.V., like a ghost vanished before our eyes.

To this day, our country never recovered from your death. When you passed away, we lost our youth. When you die, our flesh and blood became part of you. When you perish, we have landmarks that bear your name. After your death, nation turned into turmoil. There will be no other president like you.

JOHN McCRACKEN PRAYER WARRIOR

Some people in Ihop are aggressor.

Fear not John McCracken to the rescued the prayer warrior.

Never let an opportunity goes by, if any
one in need would pray over them.

People around his peer admired him and considered to be gem.

Ihoper no need to worry, John prayer is awesome.

In spiritual warfare against Satan it will be fearsome.

His message don't worry today a prayer is a day away.

Someday would meet with Jesus far away.

Prayer is best weapon on planet Earth.

Fasting and prayer at Ihop is worth.

Message of prayer conquered all negativism.

Continue communicating will spread positivism.

Someday John prayer remained us Jesus
would be knocking on the door.

When we came to Christ, gave us our yore.

In the prayer room God is returning soon.

In the future we reached to heaven in a full moon.

Need a prayer no need to worry John McCracken to rescued, brother and sister do not have a prayer don't belong in Ihop.

BY

Johnny Wong

MAGGIE MY DEAR

September of 62' was a special day, because Maggie my dear came out from my mother womb. Even though we were two years apart from each other, we have tons of fun. She is none other than my baby sister.

We played from sunrise to sunset; both were born in the Crown Colony of Britain. While everybody went to school, me and little Maggie played house. We grew up like buddies together.

We went to kindergarten together, same junior high, I carried your books, you gone to St. John University, while I attended Queens's borough Community and Queens College.

I could be the smartest person in school, but rather be by Maggie side, climbed the highest mountain or cooked the greatest meal, no greater thing being by her side. I accomplished many things in this world, instead wanted to play with her. She is my idol and will always be my buddy for the rest of my life.

MAY THE GOOD LORD LEAD YOU WITH UNEDING HAPPINESS

Today is a new day, today in a new mine, in new way, with a new wine, everyday is the same, but today is your day.

Go to sleep Alan, sleep tight, sleep wisely, sleep peacefully, lovely Elissa will sing a lullaby, sing a new song unto the Lord.

You will dream about yesterday, today and tomorrow, never stop dreaming, unto one day received a job at Nyack College, dream tree, deer, sheep, mountain, fountain, in God green pasture by the cool evening night.

May your kindness, goodness, happiness overflow others people heart with fountain of water.

Can you write us a song, a song in Jesus name, a song about Jesus love, a song written in your name, a song about reaching out to others?

As you strike each note, can your finger tell us a story in Jesus name, can it play a song in Jesus name, and can it prophesy in Jesus name, can it say a prayer in Jesus name.

The bible said "in my father house, there are many mansions, which were brought for us." Someday when you departed from planet Earth, may the Lord give you a mansion, a mansion that could not be purchased by a millionaire?

Your way lead to many friendship, yet you mention Jesus way the best.

Friendships come and go in our lives, soon it disappears, as the color of the changing leafs, but Alan friendship touches and leaves a lasting impression on others.

Lyrics taken from a Christian Song "A New Mind, A New Way."

Lyrics taken from a Christian Song "His Sheep am I."

MISTY EDWARD LYRIC'S EXCELS 2.5 MARCH

If you're lyric can fly at 2.5 march speed of sound

my writing will excel over Ihop crowd.

The day you were born magic flew in your hand.

Some day song flew to American Band Stand.

Your lyric flies F-14 Tomcat, maneuvered music as in Top Gun.

My poetic fly's a-4 sky hawks out fly you in the sun.

Fired cannon split second Jesus Christ descend.

Piano playing expressed stories of an angel being send.

Imaged piano as aircraft, key board 20 millimeter cannon, you the pilot, note book as a plane, pen a gun, I am the co-pilot.

Lyric and poetic go head in head challenge in the sky.

If song and poetic high above clouds can see each other eye.

Misty Edward ballads can out fly, out gun, out maneuvered, she has the leading edge.

With less experiences Johnny must rely on his mind, brain power to out think her opponent wedge.

One day ballads, imagery flew at 2.5 march and communicated in the sky to create a song for Ihop.

By

Johnny Wong

PANIO MAN

Today was Sunday and I am ready to head off to church. Every Sunday, I looked forward to hearing Alan plays the Piano. There's certain magic in his hands. He made the piano comes alive. It talked to us.

His mighty fingers transformed the keyboard into a mighty instrument, similar to a person singing. His loved for the keyboard was liked loving other brothers and sisters. Whenever touching the instrument, praised the lord.

Alan magical hands compared to fighting against Satan, by shooting flaming arrows and missiles at the devil. Even the sound of the instrument made Satan stayed away from us.

Mr. Rathe a very cool Christian, never showed off, or boosted about himself. He doesn't need to speak to anybody, instead let his playing do the talking. In Christian Testimony considered a one man band, playing so beautiful nobody backed him up.

I never spoke to him that often. Whenever I head off to New Jersey, he let the piano said "farewell." As I went away to Boston, the piano said "bye, bye and wished me luck." As I returned home from Hong Kong, the instrument played a happy tune. Whenever leaved or returned to C.T. the keyboard was always there to bid me farewell or said "hello." As he hit each notes, God loves poured out on us.

RENEE LOVE FOR CHILRENS

Renee the apostle Peter and John said "monies, slivers or gold I do not have." I will say the same. I'll write you a story that Jesus Christ transformed you into a beautiful princess, because of Derek compassion for the less fortunate children on planet Earth.

As Christ commanded us to come as little infants and to humble ourselves, he'll exalt us. Just as your work for the suffering of the little ones, someday, somewhere, sometime in times in Heaven, Christ set a banquet for the Derek's.

The Christian life is never easy.
It is not always based on feeling, not always how much God could reward us in this world. We might not see it at first, but during those difficult times where God searched our hearts.

Renee I don't know why God called some to go home at an early life. Today God is telling you "I loved my dear Derek so much he had served me well." "It is time for me to purchase a mansion for him in Heaven, which could not be purchased by a millionaire."

Sincerely

Johnny Wong

RESTING ON MARY'S LAP

My sister-in-law Linda was about three months pregnant. Her next door neighbor Mary asked "when is Linda going to have the baby?" "I don't know, but pretty soon." I responded.

From the look on her face, there was an radiated joy. She's adorned and loved little children'. As Jesus mentioned in the bible, "come, let the children here." In Mary mind, they're all very special.

I recalled one hot afternoon, she was so exciting to hear the arrival of the new born baby. She was sitting down, letting the baby resting peacefully on her lap. We told her, "her named was Madelyn Wong."

During those precious minutes, while Madelyn was resting on her lap, foretold a tale of Mary kindness, toward my in-law, my brother and mom.

As Madelyn was maturing in age, she would drop by sometime surprising her with cookies, gifts for taking care of their dog.

Whenever she saw me and Madelyn at the swing, would always approached us, shared a wonderful conversation with us.

When Halloween arrived she handled Madelyn a lucky quarter.

During summer time her daughter Shannon came by to baby sit and picked her up for summer camp. Around this time, she became the center of attention.

One day, I heard the sad news, it flashed liked a lighting. Mary and her family was relocating to South Carolina.

I couldn't remember when was our final conversation. Somehow I felt hurt not having her around any longer. I kept on saying "this can't be happening, wishing she will never leave us."

That day I saw the huge truck disappearing right in front of my eyes in our back yard. As the sight of the truck disappearing her memories also started to dissolve in my mind.

As I looked back on that historic day, when Madelyn was resting on her lap, it told a story concerning all of the great attributes and personalities of Mary.

We might never see eye to eye in the future, in my mind, my words will be "thank you Mary for taking care of Madelyn and giving her such a wonderful life, we can never repaid you for what you have done."

ROB THE BUCK TOOTH NEW YORKER

A guy named Rob in his mouth a buck tooth.

A kid from Chicago who's wants to preserve his youth.

Came to my apartment appear to be in hunger.

As he was dieing for some food buck tooth became dimmer.

Introduced myself to him gave me the cold shoulder.

Took out my 45 caliber, aim as a shooter.

Put a plate before his eyes, chewed it down in a hurried.

We became friends as Chinese chicken curries.

Chicago and New Yorker are the best.

When we leave I Hop meet the test.

Chicago and New Yorker hated each other.

At the same time we bad mouth each other mother.

Buck Tooth New Yorker and Johnny Wong
go to I Hop, do not have a prayer.

When I Hop girls hurt us we turned meaner.

Johnny Wong and the Buck Tooth New Yorker
eat side by side, go side by side in my diary.

laughed side by side at FSM classes, prayed
side by side in the prayer room.

BY Johnny Wong

Lyrics taken from Paul McCarty "Ebony and Ivory."

SIX GRAND FATHER LOVE'S

April 1993 at Westborough State Hospital my mom spoke to me "little duce, your six grandfather no longer around, his's gone." Those words pierced through my heart, could never imaged even to this very day, have victory over those painful words.

I love him, as the Wong family, including Gerry also had wonderful fond memories of him. We not only loved him, respected him, looked upon him as a mentor and a father figure.

I never knew why, didn't cried that night, on the other hand, difficulties falling asleep. I don't think I slept on that particular evening.

I remember maybe as a eight or a nine years old, our parents brought Simon, Maggie to his apartment. There was a wooded prank against the wall. Out of curiosity I went over, touched the object. The force was turning against my weight. Out of loved came a 70's gentle, loving, generous, nice, compassion elderly male held on to my hand, told me "son you have nothing to be afraid off, don't worry, I am always there for you."

Afterward asked mom "who was that person?" "Don't be silly little duce, that's your six grandfather, please go and thank him." Those period might be too young to understand his loved for us. Strange as it may seems, even at such a earlier age, his actions on that day, trigger a wonderful, loving bond relationship which would last for three decades.

While living on the Lower East Sides, me Simon, Maggie after school, parents told "us to spend time with him." Some circumstances he forgotten about the three of us, enjoyed playing Ma Jon." Some moments at the China Town Senior Citizens Center, we had dinner with him. The food quite enjoyable, Peking Duck, Chinese Pork, Beef, Red Snapper Fish, Sting Beans, Tofu,

Drunken Chicken, Fried Rice, White Rice, Chicken Curry with vegetables.

On warm, humid summer day, he'll take the entire family to Coney Island Beach. While growing with my siblings, those summer days, nights will forever remained in our hearts. In the 70's Coney Island the name of the place. Sight, sound, smell of salt water ocean waves, always remember summer was never far away, despised residing in New York, where angry cruel winter wind, snowing liked piled up of mountains never seems to disappear.

Six Grand Father had a hug heart for the hungry people on Earth. Whenever we came to visit, usually brought us toys and foods. As our grandfather perhaps we often took him for granted. His actions spoke louder than words. You know in this nation, all over the globe, talked is cheap, especially saying "I loved you, but failed to understand, having lack of compassion for those who are less fortunate, never reaching out to the needy, including those whose suffering. "Six Grand Father" was the exacted opposite.

Six Grand Father walked the talked, he not only spoke, but back it up demonstrated for Cindy, Suzy, Simon, me and Maggie, someday we assisted people who had very little in this world. In his heart, knew the loved he given to us, will be showed toward Nicole, Sean, Kelly, Eric, Keefe and Madelyn.

The only thing in remembered of my six grand father, was the World Book Encyclopedia, each time I picked up recalled the generosity of person whose love inspired us to enjoy, live life to the fullest. He was a giving person taught us the joy of being a cheerful giver. Never or asked any of our family to returned any favor he performed.

The greatest moment, when he saw my sister Cindy walking down the isle to meet her handsome groom. I said "the same for Simon and Linda." He also witnessed the birth of Nicole, Eric and Keefe. That's so much, wished to continued praising, giving him credits.

The last time, I spend with him was January of 93' me and my friend Phil Wan took him out for dim sum, yet he waited for over hour for me. I'll never forget the simile on his face. At the same time, during our final meal, memories of his loved for my family, Gerry, nieces and nephews just overwhelmed me. Even though at some silence moments during the meal, could sensed he concern if I'll going to make it in this world, if I could support my self finically, most importantly would I get in enough to eat.

That was our final time together, he insisted leaved down a tip. As we were leaving the restaurant, wanted, to spend some time with him, he insisted I go with Phil. Somehow I desired to say to "Six Grand Father", we thank you for gifts, your generosities, most importance, the loved you had showed to us."

He was also a very funny character, our last time even at age 93, still puffing away with the cigar, won't be surprised if he went to his apartment, had his sip of "Johnny Walker."

I had a grandfather, unlike any grandparent, who had tremendous loved for little children's. He not only spoke in love, demonstrated even while we were growing up. He never stop loving us, it never faded away either. I never had a grand father, the way he expressed himself. There will be no other grandfather to bear his name.

Farwell good bye six grand father, we're all missed you. We're cherished your memories in our heart and passed to the next generation of children's.

THANK YOU SIX GRAND FATHER !!!

STORY OF OUR TIME

Yesterday not long ago today.

Yesterday the story of our time.

Her birth children laugh and smile.

Time rock time fly

Everyday with Madelyn a time spends in Heaven.

No greater joy being by her side.

When life seems harsh remember her birth.

A moment in time.

A moment to gather by her side.

As cute and funny.

Never give Uncle Johnny a break.

I know a place where Madelyn love to boost.

In every child heart cried a sound of laughter.

Madelyn heart a treasure of love.

Madelyn birth the story of our time. by uncle Johnny

SUGAR AND SPICES

Raisin nuts, almond nuts, honey sugar crumb.

Madelyn is full of honey Cracker Jack.

Don't be moody, if loose in Black Jack.

Food is "Uncle Johnny idol."

Good food search fine soul.

Sweetly pie, honey pie, blueberry, cherry pie.

Life is full of adventure for Madelyn.

Your world is full of magic, honey, sugar and spices.

Sugary, with honey mustard cranberry.

Watery, cutie, postcard added on Madelyn birthday.

A tiny world for so many children in it.

A mighty world for wondrous stream.

Being around her, turn my world upside
down, right side up, left side down.

If there is a child, her mind is sugar and spices.

By Uncle Johnny

SUMMER IN DELIGHT

If there's a summer for Elissa, love, undivided, subtracted, from hate, anger, in addition, increased her beloved majesty royal heirless able to serve at your request.

If there's a summer for Elissa at her requested, where one could imagined the sight of green grass flowing all around, smell of Earthly ocean water, silently flowing in our imaginatively mind. The smell of hotdogs, hamburgers, chickens, with cranberry, honey comb, blazing on a streaming, flaming on a chalk coal grill.

Brids singing in the air singing in honor of your name. Sunlight shined warmed your path, foreshadowed, its light symbolized the tale of your youth. With the arrival of summer, a knight clothed in dashing armor with a crown ready to defend Elissa in her honor.

A rook over bishop, knight captured pawn, pawn attacked king, queen counter attacked bishop, rook cornered king, queen checked king, pawn checked mate king.

As summer about to end, the sun had tasted its forbidden noon. The mighty red hot flashes of organe light remained us summer days are gone, but not forgotten.

If that's the case her cute husband Alan Rathe will kissed Elissa a sweet lullaby, good night kissed.

Sincerely,

Johnny Wong

Summer of 83'

Something happened in the summer of 83 it was the thrill of my life. I and Eli purchased a six string guitar. We sang until our voice became dry. We played until our finger bleed to blood. Like Sgt. Pepper I was singing and playing out of tune when Jose taught me. When school arrived that guitar became silent. It sang a dead note to me. I locked up the guitar. It turned to snow, became white as snow. Then one day the sleeping giants awaken. Then one day its voice called out to me. "Hey Johnny could you played me a song, could you sing and danced to the beat of Elvis, write me a lyric." Are your lyrics as creative as the Beatles?" "May you harmonized to the voice of Simon and Garfunkel." As you struck the major chord, the guitar became human. Strum the minor chord it synchronized with your voice. As you played the chord it captures a story. When picking the E note every other Beatles song does excellence. A minor and B flat equaled Lennon and McCartney reactivities, G7, E minor will turned us back into the sixties. As our nation grew older my sweet guitar gently weeps. That old six string wanted to say good night to you. Sing me a lullaby and I will sleep gently. That guitar became my nubby on the summer of 83.'

Lyrics taken from Bryan Adams "Summer of 69'."

Lyrics taken from George Harrison "While my Guitar Gently Weeps."

Lyrics taken from Beatles "Sgt. Pepper Lonely Club Heart Band."

SUNDAY IDOL

For those who don't know, at the age of 11, I was die hard Mets fan. Growing up in New York, one can never be a Mets or Yankees fan. Sweating, the pain, cheering them to the last pitch, and hit was the name of the game.

Number 41 was his jersey; man name was Tom Sealer who loves to play the game. First time lay eye on him; fell in love with his pitching. He proved to us good pitching, stop good hitting.

His fearsome fast ball looked mighty awesome as each batter, foolishly went down swinging. The ball he hurled contained an angry message to any hitter who ignored its danger.

His service to honor arrived as the Mets won the World Series in 1969, when New Yorker celebrated with glory. Miracle performance in our wildest dream, as his pitching did all the talking by wining the pennant, destroying the big Red Machine during the play off.

Then something terrible happen on that autumn day, horrible as it may appear the ball no longer communicated through his hand. He fell short that day, the magic die in his hand. They were to wait anxiously, patiently, for the next 23 years, to be crowned championship again.

Screwball, fastball, breaking ball, curved ball, fork ball, spit ball, come see Sunday Idol performance to perfection.

Taken from lyrics James Taylor "Copper Line."

SWEETY PIE

Honey comb, sugar pie, heart of pleasure.

Magic pour forth, your heart full of treasure.

Cinnamon, raisin, apple sauce flowed your speech.

The refection of China Blue is as colorful as the beach.

Cheery, blueberry, strawberry sparked a charming tone.

Birds sinning, flowers blooming, trees over
landslide, is days awaking to dawn.

Velvet, rainbow, crayon towering, is toward heavenly sky.

All the color sparking brightens by the blinking of your eyes.

Spaghetti, meatball, sausage, garlic, spread on saliva.

Chicken broccoli, pork fire rice, on egg
fun young is to Mary Go diva.

Hopeless, depress, loneliness, embracing in Mary, no greater joy.

Somewhere in times when an Italian girl
married Johnny, Mary would ploy.

Life is heart breaking restlessly, greatest
moment falling on Mary arms.

As you extended your hands, lyrics echoed in jubilee.

Jesus was man from Galilee.

Will never perished until I married a Caucasian woman.

Mary they are bunch of Gold Digger will
never fall for a China man.

First step in Queens Alliance Church, sung a
song in my heart, charmed my life with

Shining emerald, created a fun place for me to
live in, turned my world upside down.

By Johnny Wong

Lyrics taken from Don McLean "Vincent."

Lyrics taken from Beatles "Lucky in the Sky with Diamond."

THANK YOU MRS. ZADAN

On Sunday while I was talking to Stan, he mentioned there were peoples and teachers who assisted us, as we matured; we wanted to thank them and find that particular person who had offered us so many wonderful things.

Stan gave me a solid advice, might never comes across that person path. On the other hand, could extend grace; comfort those who are less fortunate than we are.

Then my fifth grade teacher Mrs. Zadan came across my mind. In the beginning I didn't struck diamond, gold, oil with her.

One day she told me to put my name on the board for talking, while the class was reading. She saw me crying, could care less about me at that point, and held many angry feeling against her.

My mom gave her a very expensive Christmas present, a pin. I guessed women and girls loved jewelry, plus a box of Chinese egg roll cookies, her husband really enjoyed it, turning point emerged into wonderful, compassionate, relationship. The sky was the limited, heaven opened up; shower of blessing fell upon me.

Shared some intimacies moments with her, ashamed to say this, at the age of 12 my hormone toward her was a little high. Of the entire teacher, I had, she was the most pretty, lovely figure and tall. One day at class, I dream about her in a beauty contest, hoping she will be crown, Mrs. P.S. 13 teacher of the year.

She was always fastenings about my reading, explained to her, and enjoyed the New York Mets, Willie Mays my favorite ball player, admired military stuffs such as building model airplanes, ships and tanks.

As time flew by, I was the center of attention, even gave me a map of the planet Mars. On graduation day, she was so proud of what I accomplished.

Our final days together, she gave us a farewell kiss. As she was approaching me, I held up my hand and said "no kiss." She turned her face feeling sad. I was way too young to notice that. As I got older in life, I finally realized how hurt she was on that day. In my mind if I ever saw her, won't hesitate to kiss her.

She knew whatever I did in life, if I put my mind into it, someday I would succeed not in terms of wealth and fame. She took a young shy little innocent monster, transformed him, and knew someday he would help other in life.

Someday I am hoping of finding her, give her a kiss, said those simple words of thank you so much for handing me such a wonderful life, of all the teacher I ever encountered, she was the loveable, nicest, fun, happiness, joy store within me. There would be no other teacher to bear her name.

So much I wanted to see and thank her in person. Stan words holds true. I could never repaid for what she done for me, yet I could moved on in life, help those who were less fortunate, that's how I expressed my gratitude toward Mrs. Zadan, thank you Mrs. Zadan.

THE BIG 50

My dearest Nicole, yes today I turned into my big 50 year old birthday. I am so excited, feeling a sense of happiness over flowing in my heart.

Since I couldn't go to bed, so decided to write to you. Hey Nick, it seems strange almost our entire family birthday falls on December. Your great grand mother bra, bra, Eric, Kef, poor, poor, gong, gong, Auntie Linda, your little sister Kelly and your birthday is one week away from mime.

Today as I turned 50 years old, I though more about your and my part of our family. Yes Nick this celebration, considered to be the best birthday, I ever had, not so much in terms of getting present and monies from the Wong and Casey Clans. Contrasted to all the other birthday where I celebrated with friends, for the very first time both the Wong and Casey family was there.

Yeah, Nicky I am so sorry to tell you this "as I looked back all my years, I hadn't really lived a very good and productive live, always getting into verbal and physical confrontation.

Our life begin when we were resting peacefully with all the other babies in the large hospital room. When we were little, our parents changed our diaper.

Nicky we all have big dream and ambition to strike oil, gold, diamond, pursued the American Dream.

Nicky is never about me. The persons who influenced me the most are your Aunt Linda, Aunt Suzy, Aunt Margaret, Uncle Simon, my partner, your mom and dad, Alan, Elisa-Lin-Rate, elementary, junior, high school teachers to college professor, pastor, wife, Christian friends, all these people are the true hero.

He introduced us to a uniformed Royal Indian Army major. The major gave us a talk, instructing us about how to take precautions against air raids and bombing attacks. He also advised us about rescue operations, first aid, and firefighting in the event of bombing by the enemy. While he explained these things to us, two Gurkha junior commissioned officers (JCOs) demonstrated the methods of firefighting and the use of ordinary gadgets in rescuing the injured.

The major concluded his talk with the announcement that at twelve o'clock that day, sirens would be blown to acquaint us, as well as everyone in the town, with the air-raid signal and the all-clear signal. He told us how to take shelter immediately upon hearing the air-raid signal. He said that the all-clear signal would sound five minutes after the air-raid signal, and then we could resume our normal activities. The talk and the demonstration by the JCOs seemed somewhat like the Boy Scout drills we also did in school and roused our sense of valor and the spirit of humanitarian service.

We all waited with interest to hear the siren call, which we had never heard before. At noon on the dot, the deafening sound of sirens came from many directions and filled the air. The wailing call sounded ominous. Following the major's instructions, we lay flat on our chests with our faces down. Five minutes felt like five years.

At last, the all-clear signal sounded. This time the sound was a continuous monotone gradually fading out to a stop. As we got up, we could only exchange vacant smiles with one another, as the whole experience had put us into a mild state of shock. The teacher attempted a smile too, in an effort to express his appreciation of the disciplined manner in which we had followed the major's instructions.

The dismal effect of the siren lingered in the atmosphere of the school. Neither teachers nor students could concentrate on their studies that day. The headmaster declared an early release.

The news that Subhas Chandra Bose had established India's independent national government while he was in exile and that his troops were advancing toward the northeastern mainland of India excited the youth in India. The romance of gaining freedom from British rule enchanted them like birds in the first flash of spring. The marching song of the INA, *"Kadam, Kadam Badaya Jā"*—"March, March to Get Ahead"—became the most popular song.

Although we in school hardly had any clear idea of what freedom would be like, we felt a strange elation. For the sheer delight of it, we paraded in the playground to the rhythm of the INA marching song. Nobody encouraged or discouraged us in doing so.

The viceroy of India, Lord Linlithgow, did not consult the national leaders of India before declaring that India was fighting the Axis powers as a member of the Allied forces. While M. K. Gandhi supported British war efforts, most other leaders of the Indian National Congress Party were lukewarm. Some were clearly opposed to the idea.

As the war escalated, the British government sought the active cooperation of Indian political leaders in the war against Nazi Germany and its allies. Muhammad Ali Jinnah and the Muslim League supported British war efforts. Pandit Jawaharlal Nehru, then Congress Party president and the prospective leader of independent India, opined that India had only one army, the Royal Indian Army, which was already engaged in various fronts in the war. Until India became an independent nation and had its own army, the question of not supporting the war would be only a precipitative gesture.

My father, who regularly listened to the Indian State Broadcasting Service (ISBS) English newscast at nine p.m., now listened to the BBC newscast at ten p.m. for more details of the war. After midnight, he secretly listened to some other foreign radio broadcasts in the privacy of his bedroom. Father never discussed politics or war but was visibly concerned at the day-to-day developments within and beyond the country.

Excitement and tension engulfed the entire nation. People in Assam generally were alarmed at the news that the forces of the INA, along with Japanese forces, were advancing in the northeast frontier areas. They were worried about possible devastation if the Japanese army advanced farther into the Indian mainland.

A regiment of the Allied army descended on my hometown carrying their armaments and outfits in convoys of trucks, jeeps, and vehicles of various shapes and sizes. They made the town's Victoria Memorial Park their command post. The popular public garden overlooking our school and the

Not much changed during my 50th. I lived in the house, similar to most ordinary houses, grew up and played in the same neighbor, yet I considered this birthday the best, even if I had not received any monies or gifts from my sibling and in-laws.

On this day, also remembered a very remarkable woman, fifth grade teacher Mrs. Linda Zadan. She's always believed in me, through her words and action, never sell short of myself. She knew if I put my mind into it, I'll be successful, not in terms of wealth and fame, but extending grace to the less fortunate.

On my 50th birthday these all the people who had either impacted, touched or made a better world for me, today they are my true hero. Thank you all.

Sincerely

Johnny Wong

THE CANADIAN INVADED IHOP

It is true every Canadian are born in skates.

If every day Weldon and Lout it will have
Chinese food on their plate.

When it comes to hockey American and
Canadian are arch rivalries.

I will be extremely exciting if most
Canadian medals was deliveries.

First step at I hop they poisoned us with
their good Canadian manner.

If U.S. beat Canada for Good loose your sweeper.

U.S. and Canada boosted in strafing the big bucks.

Weldon escaped to I hop, to see the ducks.

If New Yorker attitude was bad, Canadian was one step behind.

Some how Weldon loved to intimate the
New Yorker Boston Accent.

Weldon and Lout it loved to express their warm and wholeness.

If Weldon said "every Chinese restaurant operated to its fullness."

While at I hop he always mentioned if I opened a Chinese restaurant will be a millionaire.

Bill Gates had already outsmart the Chinese restaurant, so he's a billionaire.

On this day Canadian emerged with a fellow New Yorker, with a prayer at I hop was not for behind.

The Element of Life

Dear Pat, the day you came forth, the
element of life was discover.

While testing in your crib the discovery
of DNA molecule was engineer.

As you learned about DNA Adenine and Thymine.

Learning to speak, Guanine and Cytosine was communicating.

In preschool, the molecule-double Helix was developing.

Playing with dolls and house Chromos in the nucleus was form.

Once in adolescent, your life function in nucleic acid.

Upon graduation from high school your journey
translated by Ribose-Nucleic-Acid.

College graduation your day be blessed by Adenine.

Your first day be full of Thymine.

On your wedding day DNA Helix be a joker.

First kissed of Tim turned into fire cracker.

THE FLYING MACHINE

They called me the fighting Falcon. I am one mean flying machine. I would obeyed your commanded, flew at the speed of sound carried deadly weapons with me armed with Sidewinder missiles, 20 mm. cannon, laser guided bombs, happened to be the best in the world.

Any aircraft that wanted to challenge, would be destroyed, flew like a Falcon, was born in 1976, sold to Saudi Arabia in exchanged for foreign oil. Our country was to later on to regret. As a fighter jet, I am also a member of the Air Force, the Blue Thunder. They flew in formation and performance difficult stunts. People cheered, smiled, applauded, when performance to perfection in an air show. During those days you captured the heart of many people. We were proud of being an American.

Then in 1981, was called to duty, due to tension in the Middle East. On that hot summer day, went a dangerous suicidal mission to destroy a nuclear power plant, before it was constructed in Iraq. Once again, my nation drafted me into action during the Gulf War of 1991. As long as I am alive the mighty Falcon will fly and fight in honor of the United States Air Forces.

THE GARBAGE WRITER

Hi, everybody my name is David. They call me the "Garbage Writer." I write whatever comes into my mind. I do not care too much about grammar, because it prevents me for writing.

I take a topic out from the blue and transform it into real life. Unlike other writer, the garbage writer has no fancy words, sentences or standard format. He is like a basketball player who picks up the entire loose ball and makes something happen. His world is full of junks, old, and rusted.

The garbage writer is not afraid of anybody. He will fight to preserve his writing. You give him a day work and he will make things happen. He lives in a world which has no beginning or ending.

Once he has inks in his hand, the garbage writer will not surrender or die. He will write in honor of his name. To those who want to stop him, you must take away his pen. He will continue writing tile the day he die.

THE GREATEST HOSTESS IN KANSAS CITY

Words like endless rain flowing in my heart.

Mary tenderness tickles a lasting impact.

"Johnny how can we provide"

During my stay in Kansas City things would exceed.

Journey seeks lost soul.

She's a hostess with band of gold, ready to comfort you.

Soft as an angel, God created an image.

An image of a heavenly angel.

A picture is worth a thousand words.

Her action holds a thousand meaning.

You're the one Jesus cherish.

You're the one that I admired.

Assisting me in Kansas City.

Jesus first miracle in Canaan.

True love rings a sweet accord.

Blackbird singing at the crack of dawn.

Hostess, pot roast, egg roll, chicken roll, finger roll.

Snack times, meal times, evening times.

Any time of the day she would nourishes your soul.

One can never go hungry on Norton Road.

She's the hostess with a band of gold,
waiting to bless you in Kansas City.

By Johnny Wong

Lyrics taken from Bully Holly "Peggy Sue Got Married."

The Rich Girl of I hop

Danielle, Cornell, Chanel, you're the rich girl of I hop.

My eyes caught fired, when I saw your convertible.

Is your convertible lease able.

At I hop I never had a car.

Your car shined liked star.

For I never knew Danielle.

If returned to I hop, could I get a ride on your convertible.

Beautiful, blonde haired Danielle.

Joyful, lovely, named rhymed as a bell.

Pretty golden feature sparked liked Chanel.

Sweet honey fragrance stored in a gel.

If you're rich girl, why at I hop?

The wealth you possessed nobody at I hop can top.

Seeing your designer jeans, and jewelries
one could only obsessed.

If you are rich, only rich girl lived in castle.

You might not liked Chinaman, so you yell.

Don't be a fool, someday you will fell.

An expensive parcel will arrived at your door.

Someday, will married a wealthy Chinaman.

This man happened to be C.E.O.

Living on the peak of Hong Kong.

Playing Ping Pong with King Kong.

Having Chinese food everyday.

From Johnny Wong

THE TWO LITTLE RASCALS

On the night of December 24, 1991 born the two little rascals, the two little rascals are twin. They lived in the world of adventures. Their world is full of toys, such as horses, knights, bishops, Kings and Queens.

People wherever you are, rich, poor, happy, sad, angry, come play with the two little rascals. Put all your problems aside, take my hand and we will have the times of our life. The little rascals, brighter your days take away your sorrow and replace it with joy.

My name is Eric. I am one of the twins. I love to sit on people lap. I love to eat ice-cream. I like to run, make people smile. My name is Keefe, I am the little brother. I desire to make noise, so people can laugh. I want to play hide and seek.

My world is your world, and your world is our world. We will turn it upside down; make the clock go backward, so we have more time to spend with our mommy and daddy. The rascals have all the time in the world and they would like to spend it with you.

Day after day, they go to the play ground. Eric enjoys the swing, while Keefe likes the seesaw. Eric likes to shoot marbles, Keefe desire to run around. They both admire playing with animal.

Time after time the rascals would want to cherish their precious moment with everybody. Their universe has no beginning, no ending. At nighttime their universe transform into a beautiful scene. Every night they put on a show for us to watch. Once the little rascal matures into adulthood their world will be handed over to other babies and children's. Eric and Keefe universe will reign forever and nothing will stop them.

Taken lyrics from Bee Gees "My World."

Taken lyrics from James Taylor "Up on a Roof."

This poem is for a girl named Elizabeth who's suffer a seizure in Kansas City

SOME DAY FOR ELIZABERTH

Someday, somewhere, somehow out of heaven, a day of comfort, a day of wisdom, a day you will be free from your pain.

A day together we shine in Jesus name.

A day, a brand new day where you can start out new.

The day you were suffering, I turned felt your pain.

In a crowded room Jesus reached out his hand to you.

Oh Elizabeth, oh Elizabeth, I believe, we believe, you believe Jesus can performance a miracle.

Not long ago seems like yesterday.

Yesterday you accepted Christ the greatest miracle.

The day you departed from Earth, final miracle.

Here comes the sunshine, here comes the Savior.

Heaven lift up your name.

Jesus extends his hand.

Memories of your pain will be gone.

Lyrics taken from Elton John "Someday out of the Blue."

TO OLD CHAP

Maggie my dear our games were simple.

We scribble for bubble.

Play tilt sunrise to sunset.

As we grew older, we carried our asset.

School, was not our interest.

Found it to be humorist.

You learned the alphabet.

Both struggled with arithmetic.

You loved for English expanded.

I needed to be depended.

Ice cream and soda your sweetheart.

My favorite snack was pop tart.

Elementary to college graduated same year.

People hurt us in life, shared tears.

We had angry words in life.

Our angry moments cut liked a knife.

A minute in time with Maggie was a minute in birth.

Growing up with Maggie was my best childhood memories.

By Johnny Wong

TOMB OF AN UNKNOW SOLIDER

There is something special concerning this Memorial Day. On this day, we paid tributes to those who perish during the war. Today honored the Tomb of an unknown solider.

Quieting inside the tomb, he tells us a story. The day my mother gave birth to me I became a solider. I was born to be a solider.

While the war was rarely in Vietnam I volunteer to fight, to protect the freedom of my country. For those who don't know me, I am an unknown solider, fighting in an unknown war, dieing in an unknown course, living in an unknown land. A soldier with out a name.

WALKING GIANT

Once up-on of time in America laid the site of an unknown
solider, fighting in unknown war, dieing for an unknown cause.

For this month we celebrated the war veterans in our country.
Our country was also my family and your country also mine.

Not long ago, a walking giant emerged on this
planet. Yet he never picked up a sword or a rifle.
In his heart a hidden treasure of love.

In his mind he fought evil with good.

A story shines in his name like Robin Hood.

A knight in flashing armor for her heiress.

A story in honor of his mighty fortress.

As a little boy he carried the faith of a mustard seed.

Yet he's motivated, to practice his creed.

Whenever receiving gift always had a heart of gratitude.

Assisting a lost Chinese girl would be true longitude.

Ocean apart, steam of honey melting inside of him.

Being born in this month echoed a Chinese-Irish folk tale.

Solider fought, solider died in honor of their country.

His birth in honor of my family.

In my wildest dream, the Walking Giant
inherited most of his dad greatness.

On Memorial Day America cherished the unknown solider.

Let the Wong and Casey Clan celebrate for this
month the Walking Giant Sean Casey was born.

From Uncle Johnny

Your Name full of Honey

Nicole, Nicole, sweet, honey darling.

Dreaming on a Saturday night.

Do not be afraid of the dark.

Be on your mark, Uncle Johnny will composed.

Stay closed to your dream.

Ring around roses, dream turned to reality.

Stars, moons, skies, stream on a show.

For tonight you would find your love.

As twilight approached a handsome prince descended.

Circle of flowers surrounded you and serenaded.

You're full of honey in a jar.

In a land in another time, you're a sweetheart.

He will serenaded you with a melody.

Let not your heart be afraid, nobody jeopardized.

Mountain, fountain, no other name as sweeter than Nicole.

No other girl as fame, and charmer than Nicole.

From Uncle Johnny

Taken from lyrics James Taylor "Never die Young."

A GENEOUS WOMAN

I recalled during the autumn of 83', loan a hundred dollar for my sister boyfriend to pay back his student loan. Well when it comes to monies, especially in America, they said "there's no free lunch." I was pretty demanded to get my monies back.

Suzy my second oldest sister had no choice, but to chase him. After receiving it back, a big relieved. That was not the end of the tale. My mom gave me a solid advice, when giving don't have high expectation from people.

She's explained a wonderful story to me, concerning a very nice woman, who gave out of her heart. It was the summer of 1972, we were too poor to purchase a plane ticket to visit my grandmother in Hong Kong. Mrs. Lee Out of her gracious heart, loaned the monies so me and my mom could fly to Hong Kong.

Never knew the exact timing in repaying Mrs. Lee the monies, guessed it took about three years. Out of her heart, never once demanded or rush in paying back. After finally receiving the cash, her amazing of respond was "wow I am in no rush to received your monies, you're sure don't need it for something else."

My major difficulties arise, give too much, expecting high in return. Now a day, also needed to cut back in giving, even among closed friends and family members.

One thing that did hurt me most during my stay at I hop while cooking, giving monies to these White suburban girls, just remember you for short period of time, when ever encountered them on face to face basis, simply showing no gratitude at all.

One brother at I hop from Georgia said "the Asian people give out of their heart, us White folk, grabbed it without any gratitude."

My expiation to him "please don't demand not all White folks are greedy, selfish or self-center."

I don't mean to put judgment on any I hop girls, maybe too young to understand when having great wealth. One Christian brother shared with me "Johnny look at it this way when Jesus healed the nine leapers, how many came back and returned thank?"

Sometime, I needed to step down from receiving praise, pride and regenerations from people. If people said "I am generous" is nothing what Johnny Wong boosted about, but God gave me that gift.

My definition of giving is not how much can we received from God, but despised even going through difficulties circumstances, comforting and extending grace to others is true give, again not asking anybody to agree, each had their opinions.

Another person taught me the meaning of giving was Paul Nash, very generous with his time, monies in extending grace to individuals. One day told him "I don't have a job, too poor to ever repaid you." "You know what Johnny someday when you could help those who are less fortune than you are, that how you repaid me."

Those exact words I said to my nieces and my nephews.

As I finished writing this letter, please prayed for me, someday I too wanted to be like that generous woman Mrs. Lee Who taught the true meaning of giving.

Sincerely

Johnny

CHRISTMAS AND HANUKKAH

Christmas celebrated on the 25th, while Hanukkah celebrated a week before.

Hanukkah was observed by the lighting of the candelabrum. It is observed for eight nights.

Christmas is the birth of Christ. I guessed me and Julie had many things in common.

Me being a Christian celebrated Christmas, while she celebrated Hanukkah.

Julie as a little girl dream of having a feast with her family.

On the 24th the Wong and Casey families all get together for a Christmas eve dinner.

In my family we sang Christmas Carol, while her family sang Hanukkah songs.

Her family was from Russia, my family from China.

None of us grew up wealthy. On Christmas and Hanukkah, we dreamed of a better world, where we strifed on family value, health, hard work and prosperity.

On Christmas I dreamed of receiving as mush toys as possible.

On Hanukkah Julie dreamed of someday counseling people. Whenever is Christmas or Hanukkah Julie is always proud of my writing,

I am also proud of Julie, she's my counselsor, we don't always see eye to eye, but in a world of volience, hate, racism anger, evil, Julie always strifed there's hope, tomorrow, will be a better world for both of us.

By Johnny Wong

JOHNNY' WORLD

My world is consist of junks, broken images, broken objects, metals and full of garbage's. With the tip of my pen, commanded this stuffs into a human being. A story, fantasy world, in which captured the imagination of an audience.

A writer world make up of fantasies, ideas, creativities, emotions, feelings, poetries, music, and lyrics.

Grammars, spellings, punctuations, commas are importance to any writer, on the other hand please do not let these things prevent you from being creativities and imaginative.

A writer universe has no beginning or ending. My writer world started, a spring day of 1987, Elissa-Lin-Rathe told me to keep a diary.

Eva this is the made believed world of Johnny Wong'. What is your world?

MIRACLE ON ICE

Every true Canadian a hockey player.

Beware if American upset be true marker.

In hockey Canadian and U.S. to be worst enemies.

The two nation cannot afforded any retiree.

In any Olympic Canadian team meet the quest.

Don't be surprised if their weakness in their nest.

In 1968 Hockey Canada became professional.

Birth of Canadian Hockey shined international.

The junior hockey was also established.

As young kid emerged to stardom their blood bleed.

During the Olympic game Canadian the conqueror.

Wining the gold medal was their laborer.

A skate with a ticket to view the show.

Every Canadian born with stake to go with the flow.

In military jet March 1 breaking the sound barrier.

In hockey the pluck fly liked a Harrier.

Winning championship proved to be a miracle on ice.

If their lyrics could be sung as American Pie.

MY DAD

I believed when I was in the eight grade, as I was getting ready to wake up for junior high school, could hear his footstep across the floor. Those days, too young to noticed how tried he was. He worked in the Chinese restaurant, from 6 p.m. to 6 a.m., must be very exhausted coming home.

During my teenage years, counter many anger words from him. He always wanted people to pity him, having a very low self-esteem. In returned gave the whole family a very low esteem. For so many years hated him for that, in my mind usually quote "why can't you just accepted yourself and be proud of who you are in society, when people come to this country, not mastering the English language, that the only kind of work they could found." "Why are you always ashamed of who you are?" I asked him.

As I grew older, I fully understood he had a terrible childhood, he never did had a father, when he was four years old, his dad died, leaving my grandmother who happened to be very strict with him. Not possessing a father figure, he never knew how to love us.

At age fourteen, he had to leave his family, behind, unlike New York or the State where there's public transportation, in China one must travel long miles to seek employment.

Due to many anger confrontations with him, developed an very unpleasant anger, trouble individual, recalled one incident, while at age ten or eleven took out a butcher knife to scar both of my oldest sisters, they told him, even to this day out of his kindness, told me nicely not to do it again.

I remembered crying for him at I hop, labeling it as a waste of time, false humilities, putting on an act. You see Asian people, especially the Chinese considered to be S.O.B. crying was a huge failure, even among women. If you were to take a White and

Chinese, most likely the Caucasian girl if she's sad, hurt or joyful, usually will cried.

As I returned from Kansas City there were more verbal, nasty and violence confrontation between me and him. Afterward I told John I hop was a big waste of time, things weren't going very smoothly in New York, though I was going to marry a nice Caucasian girl and lived the American Dream in Kansas City, his responded "was I got some healing at I hop, stop struggling with my feeling and moved on with my life."

In February seeing the movie "Dear John" in regard of his dad having a mental illness, guessed what I shed some treats for my own dad again. At the end of the movie, headed over to the department store, purchased a small gift for him.

From that day on I said to myself "my dad is getting very old, I'll never let anybody take him to die in a nursing home, I desired me and my family to take care of him. Sorry for such a long painful story, this is the story of my dad and I am proud of him.

From

Johnny Wong

IS NEVER "UNCLE JOHNNY"

Dear Nicky and Kelly, my writing, gift of music, monies, possessions of materials things, whatever I had in life, my generosities, friendliness, comforting others never belong to uncle Johnny. God gave me all these, I own none of them.

Everything I had in life belongs to Nicole and Kelly. I do not feel right in taking credits for it. I encouraged my nieces to always showed thankfulness in what they had, never take things for granted. Both your dad and mom worked real hard to give you the best in life.

My message, is true we have to take care of our own needs in order to help others. On the other hand, if we're always concerned about our situations, indulging in self-pity, then we became a salve for everybody to assisted our own problems.

I challenged individuals despite our suffering, please take a good looked at a world, where millions of children's going to bed hungry, living in the cold, enduring the mighty heat, during the summer times.

Gratitude or being thankful is not so much asking for a payback or a favor, but if what we could reached out to those less fortunate than we are. Talk is very cheap when showing lack of love in meeting physical and mental pains to a world which is suffering.

Too many fundamentalist, chiasmic born-again Christians boost how much they loved God. Too many times, I heard too many testimonies "oh god been so good to me, he gave me a good job, beautiful wives, making a six figure salaries, living the American Dream, I loved him, just wanted to praise him."

I don't even liked the term born-again, just a fancy jargon, used during the 1976 election. The question if God, never given all these above gifts, in your heart, do you still said "God is good, I loved him or praises him.

Please I know we're not perfect, there's a difference between judging and correcting. Too many born-again used the slogan "oh you should judge Johnny, please examined your life. You know whoever said this "I agreed your statement, most, but not a hundred percent."

You know how much I loved my nieces, if people said or do anything inappropriate, making them feel uncomfortable I have very right to defend or protect from any them form any harm. That is not judging, but correcting the individuals, judging is when I used physical, talking aggressively, using foul language, then that believers have very right to called it judging, because I wasn't doing it in loved.

Looked everybody, my main weakness, Pastor Wendell always said "Johnny you're not the policeman of other people actions." He usually stated my expectation on people are way too high." "To this day I agreed with him." When sharing my faith with individuals, I also gave them the dark side of "Johnny Wong." People do not liked to be shock or surprised by anybody.

Going back to Nicole and Kelly, I did a lot bad, evil things, made quite a few poor decision in life. I never desired them to followed my footstep, there's a wonderful world waiting for both of you, so pleased lived life with joyful smile to its fullest. Good Night.

NORMANDY DIARY

During the invasion of Normandy, a British solider kept a diary in his head. As I walked though endless raindrops, feeling the cool summer breeze, sweating liked a hunger dog. The mighty sound of heavy artillery, noises of reckless bombing and shelling, witnessing men falling to their death.

While I could hear the wounded shouting, crying in agony in pain. Many of these soldiers begging, pleading to God to have mercy on them, if they could get by another day.

I assumed just getting by another day, not only for individuals in the Arm Forces, but for those who are mentally ill or physically disable, considered a big step for us.

In every Fourth of July, as our beloved nation celebrated Independence Day, we also have a right to be recognized importance individual.

As the Declaration of Independence stated that "all men are created equated, we who are disable also are created equal too."

Sincerely

Johnny Wong

The War With in Us

All war lead to hell. In every conflict, there's causalities on both sides. When that's fighting everyone, including civilians labeled as causalities of war.

During the Second World War, the strategic bombing of both sides, the Axis and the Allied, considered to be very tragic as hundred, thousand and millions innocent civilians die.

Somehow we asked ourselves, "what is the purpose of war?" Where individuals killing, suffering, dieing for who knows what?

Some may wonder was the Second World War justify? I myself do not liked hated, violence and the spread of evilness.

Some Allied commanders insisted in bombing Nazi Germany and Imperial Japan to surrender, even though killing many civilians as possible. Many people argued "it was these two nation which started the war, let's destroyed their cities and industry might."

My opinion on World War Two was necessary to stop the spread of evilness. Most people didn't knew, when we had the Atomic Bomb, was going to use it on Germany, but she surrender, before Japan did. I think Thurman made a wise decision by ordering the bomb to drop on Japan, because her people will not surrender, they said "they're fight to the last men."

I'll also liked to talk about a difference kind of conflict and that is the war within us. Whenever that's hate, rage, jealously, vengeance and anger though we ourselves are not much better than modern combat solider fighting against each other.

Angry, curse words in somewhere, labeled as a form of weapon to hurt one another feelings. Symbolized as sword, knife, rifle, machine guns and bullet intended to wound or injured the other.

One of the most powerful arsenal is our tongue. Whenever people mention "sticks and bone may hurt me, but words will never hurt me." I considered that to be a big joke, words are powerful. If used in a negative way, could scared you for life.

Sincerely

Johnny Wong

WE CAN'T CHANCE PEOPLE HEART, BUT
WE CAN CHANCE IN OUR OWN HEART

I recalled living in Boston, Massachusetts for about five years, many Blacks little kids, teenagers, including adults made a lot racist remarks toward me. Out of all the places, I lived most of the racism came from the town of Arlington, Massachusetts, Anglo, Catholic White folks, Blacks and Chinese treated me like a piece of dirt.

First sign of racism came from an Anglo-White couple who didn't liked Chinese people, while I was painting their house. Cheerleaders made fun of me, trying to speak Chinese. A fellow named Tim from the Chinese take out order and his crew were all shouting in Cantonese to "fire me." A Black fellow came, lived with us, never paid utilities, rent, maybe even stole my camera. Disagreement with my landlord, evicted me. Blacks guys were kicking my chair, saying racist remarks to me while taking the bus. Teenagers girls, in the restaurant making racist remarks and ridiculing my Chinese New York accent. Punched a Black bus driver, the white Women and male dispatcher forced me to talk, without counseling an attorney for me. Got into a fight with a racist Black and White male at the subway station.

About every other week Afro-Americans boys, girls, teen ridiculed me with their racist remarks. Even to this very day, arriving to this state Afro-Americans showed direct or indirect racism against me. One Chinese company manager will keep on making excused not to hire me.

To this very day, still have a lot of hatred and anger against the state of Massachusetts, I still held a lot of vengeance especially against the town of Arlington Massachusetts. Though out my entire life in Massachusetts, I had found no real joy or peace from the evilness, racism, anger, violence, a lot of hatred from all these group of people who treaded me with such cruelty.

When I asked my pastor Wendell, "as Jesus was riding on the donkey on Palme Sunday, was it the exact same people who cried crucify him one week later?" All the people shouting at the top of their voice "Hosanna is the king of Israel" was it the very same people one week later shouted "crucify him." Wendell said "it was the exact same people."

Yet at the same time when I witnessed how much Jesus suffered for my sins. I had never gone through some of the suffering both emotionally and physically of Christ, his disciples and the early Christians missionaries. Jesus was whipped with a steel rod for about 40 times, Romans soldiers slapped, spat at his face, ridiculed him, put a thorn crown on his head. Forced him to carry the cross, while hanging at the cross, they hurled insulted at him, commenting" if you're the son of Christ, come down and we're believed, he saved others, but not himself."

On that Good Friday, he extended grace, compassion, loved, plus a quality of mercy for whoever willingly to acknowledged their sins and accepted him by faith.

I am not ready yet, on the other hand I prayed someday, God if you're have me returned back to the town of Arlington, Massachusetts and tell this people about the love of Christ, no matter how long or how many years it take.

Dear God our heavenly father I can't chanced the people heart in the town of Arlington Massachusetts or the city of Boston. As for Johnny Wong, he could chanced his own heart, very, very, very easy to say, but hard to do.

Wonderful Kelly

Wonderful Kelly, if I could tell you a story.

Written in a mansions that could not be purchased.

Remembered in times, a vision came into place.

Remembered your birth, a nation struggled to survived.

Countrymen, king, queen, prince and princess at your request.

Give me a pen, a piece of paper at your conquest.

Oh Kelly, my beautiful, lovely, darling Kelly, full of honey.

> Today, today, my beautiful Kelly, no word
> rhymed as honey, lovely beautiful angel.

> God created angel and he created in style,
> one of them happened to be Kelly.

Kelly full of cheery, if I could baked you a blueberry.

A king and a knight at your mission.

They traveled information.

By uncle JohnnyA

SYMPHONY FOR ELISSA

Your birthday may the joy of music
surrounded by guitar fingerboard.

Lyrics, melodies, symbolized the refection of motherboard.

Treble clef notes Christ dwelled Elissa folly goodness.

Bass clef centered devoting falling holiness.

A guitar sting Elissa boldness gracious dedicated electrify.

C major chord courageous exciting conductivity.

G major chord greatness, beautiful gatherers.

Every notes, chord resembles together.

Beethoven, Mozart, Shubert, Bach, a sting quartet.

Elisa counseling others is her novelist Burnett.

Your birthday Lennon and McCarty sung a harmonic interval.

Brian Adams, Christopher Cross, Richard
Max, Phil Collins at your referral.

Amy Grant, Keith Green, Larry Norman,
Randy Stone Hill your greatness contest.

Michal W. Smith, Twilight Paris, Maratha
Singers, Honey Tree at your quest.

Alan playing harmonic and melodic interval on your arrival.

Brother John, Jingle Bell, Merrily We Roll,
Mary Ann, Carrie Ann, a holy roller.

Hark the heralds, Angels we heard on high,
away in a manger, a Christmas Carol.

Caroline, Jacqueline, Madelyn, Carissa, Elissa,
Melissa, baby songs at institute.

Every girl loves to charm, every girl loves to pray.

As a little baby, a flute sung as she's shared.

Eine Kleine Nachtmusik, joyful, joyful we adore,
Jesus Joy of Man Desired written in pleasure.

A flute, trumpet, French horn, drumming
to the sound of leisure.

Violin, bass, cello, sting quartet, flowing in endless images.

A picture worth a thousand words, a diary worth
a thousand meanings, music rhyme the soul.

An orchestras, a symphony in delight in a stroll.

Monies, fame, world possessions only temporary,
the gift of writing cherished in our heart.

On her birthday Elissa had given the greatest
gift in the world. Sincerely, Johnny WongDiary
of an American solider in Normandy

Dear Mary heart of gold, lips as sweet as cheery. Face full of pink
daisy. Smiled radiated liked sunflower. Today was June 6, 1944, I
am writing this diary to you on a landing craft bounded for the
invasion of Normandy France. Our supreme Allied commanders,
Anglo-Americans label this day as D-Day, meaning "Dooms Day."

Eisenhower, gave us a prep rally announcing this to be our greatest
day in history, because we were going to returned France to
liberate its people from Nazi occupied Germany. Their leaders,
their nations, people waiting years to be free. He warned us some
or most of us will not returned, most likely be killed by enemies
fired. He desired each of us to do there utmost duties, services for
the Americans people back home. He stated "our job, considered
to be very vital in defeating Hitler Nazi Germany in brining to
the war to the end." "Even though most of you will be perished
before you hit the beach of Normandy, on the other hand go and
give them hell." He said. "Today our beloved country United States
people back are mighty proud of you."

Dear Mary our target co-named Omaha Beach. In the background,
I could hear the mighty thundering of 16, 14 inch. Gun of our
battleship, its shell roaring on the beaches of Normandy. As I viewed
the sky the flares of rockets, liked Fourth of July fire work racing
toward the sandy beaches. As I turned my eyes to the left, I saw
Dauntless Dive Bomber, p-51 Mustang, and p-47 Thunderbolt fighter
armed with bombs ready to unleashed on the enemies artilleries.

Dear Mary we're about half way to the beaches. I am very nervous and scared. What happened if I don't made to the beach? What happened if our mortal shells or artilleries shell landed on our landing craft killing all of us? What happened if I get shot by a sniper?

"O.K. men this is it, let's moved it out." Shouted the lieutenant. "Mary I am going to put this diary away in my body, for now on, going to communicated through my mind."

Once the landing craft dropped their door, I witness men around me helplessly, rapidly falling face down to meet their terrible ordeal, Eisenhower was absolutely correct many of us were killed by German machines guns bullets and mortal, artilleries shells. They were killing us similar as practicing as shooting galley. I could see arms bodies flying all over the places. Bloods spreading on the beaches, friends, buddies crying out in agonies. Mary this is no dramas or faction, this is not a movie, this is war and in real combat, men killing each other.

Mary please asked God to spare my life, if he could get me out of this mess, I promised I won't gambled, won't have sex, won't smoked, no longer get into physical or verbal confrontation with any bodies. I will never tasted the smell of alcohol beverages'. I will still wished to marry you and be the best handstand in life.

By two to three hours, everything was over, the whole ordeal finished. We finally secured the beach head. Unfortunately casuistries were very high over 2,000 men killed or wounded. It took us a couple of more hours to bury our dead comrades.

By night fall, as tried as we happened to be, we slowly inch step by step to reach the city of Paris. At dawn one could hear the sound of birds if they were sinning. We all felt the chill of the morning frost. Light rain gently fell among us. The strong smell of our odor, let us know when is time for a shower. Within the next hours sunlight radiated, symbolized there's hope for each men, made a shiny path for us to guide us to victory.

Later on we dug fox hole in wait for the enemies to arrived. I decided to take my diary, once again wrote to Mary. "Dear Mary thank God I had made it this far." "I have a good feeling I am going to survive this terrible war." "I had seen men dieing, many of them crying in pain." "On the other hand our morale is very high." "We all loved to go to see that beautiful city called Paris." "The French civilians was very kind, nice and generous to us, they offered shelter and foods for many of us." "Without their assistance, it might be very hard to get by." "Have you get a chance to say hi to my parents, brothers and sisters?" "Are you going to have a delicious supper tonight?" "The French Farmers feeds us quite well, they gave us chickens, cheese, steaks, French bread and pasties with milk to drinks." "I am sorry Mary once again, I must put away my diary, needed to prepared to wait upon the enemies."

Then suddenly without any warning a mortal shell landed on top of his foxhole, one fellow soldiers saw him groaning in pain. He shouted "medic come here, we have a wounded solider in pain." He started to whisper to himself my God, what hit me, why is this happening, what exactly when wrong? "Don't worry Private, let me check you out, I'll tried my best to save you. "Don't brother I don't think anybody could save me, not even you." The solider responded. "I know who can save you that's God and Jesus Christ." "I been a good person in life and I go to mass and confession almost every Wednesday and Sunday." "Private we're not going to Heaven, because of our good work, instead we're going to Heaven

by what Christ did for us on the cross and repented of our sins."
"Do you want to ask Christ to come to your heart?" "Yes I do."
"My diary in my back pocket, please made sure it gets to my girl
friend back home Mary." "Yes I made sure it will." Then the soldier
closed his eyes and passed away. The medic took his hand and said
"thank God you're in peace and in heaven right now, please rest
in peace.My love for Sean

As a little two years old, he showed his love toward his uncle by
extending his arms to him. While eating Chinese Marconi with
soup and hot meats, aunt Margret ask him "Sean you want more?"
His responded was mum, mum."

As he matured in life, I knew he will carried the inherited the
wonderful attributes, personalities of his dad.

At age 8 or 9 he demonstrated a lot of love toward me, when he
said "not all Black people are bad." Something about him, he
always had love, affection for people regardless, of race, gender
or religion.

He always had a thankful heart, no matter how small the gift was.
"Uncle Johnny" might not accomplished much in life, on the other
the achievements he strife for simply amazed me.

One funny episodes during his sixteen birthday, in a Chinese restaurant, the waitress handed him a folk. Sean stared at her with no expression, wasn't a pleasant looked on his face. "I guessed in his mind, why's wrong with you Chinese people you don't think us White folks know how to use chop-stick." Afterward I told the waitress, he's half Irish, half Chinese, today is his birthday. She felt so embarrassed right a way she's apologized, also wished him a happy birthday.

Before he left for Annapolis, had a quite moment together. Told him "I always dreamed of going to the Naval Academy, become a hotshot navy pilot landing and taking of from the flight deck of the U.S.S. Enterprise. By age 16 started to wear glasses, so my chanced fade into the divine wind. Still tried to enlisted a couple of times, but due to my mental illness, I withdrawal myself from going into the Navy.

Today I am mighty proud of the achievements he made. Just said "he meet my dream."

Sincerely,

Uncle Johnny

THERE'S A HALLOWEEN IN ALL OF US

No matter how young being two, four, six, teenagers, adults and elderly, senior citizens, physical or mental disability, normal individuals, there's a Halloween in all of us. All group of this people even titled to go Trick O' Treat.

As little girls and little boys our parent brought customs for us. Little boys dream of wearing cowboy suits, showing off their fancy six shooters, while some dressed up liked Indians. While some put on military uniform, maybe to follow their dad footstep.

Well can't never counted little girls out of the picture, they're importance. Little girls similar to my niece Kelly dress up as little princess like "Snow White" or beautiful mermaid. May be some boys loved to be Knight in shining armor, and girl dream on Trick O' Treat, dress as a pretty, beautiful Queen as your "Royal Heirless."

My first Trick O' Treat started around October 31, 1972 with my baby sister Maggie. Even though Maggie was two years behind me, we're played with each other, for elementary to college. It was my first and only Halloween Night together with her.

By that time, me and Maggie collected monies for Unified to help children's fight against poverties. Whenever my neighbor put in a penny, seeing a smile on their face, still hold fond remembrance of my first and only Halloween with Maggie. Over all me and little Maggie collected closed to a hundred pennies. The day after Halloween our class, boosted how much each individuals collected monies for hungry children's.

The only thing I am against kids no matter how young they're should not, never, never, never throw eggs at people, which is very cruel, evil, because in many countries, including many children and adult are starving in this world. I knew and understood what hunger was liked in my family, three sisters, an older, if you're late for dinner, only a bowl of rice left.

For those who don't know "Johnny Wong" might over extended myself too much, having high expectations of others. Some days, I could the nicest in the world, next day could be a very angry sob. In cartoon Luck gave Charlie Brown a rock for Trick O' Treat, if any body gave Johnny rock, I suggested better run day for day light and an apology, if you don't believed me called my pastor and his wife, they're be nice enough to give you an answer.

As you can see, looking back my first and only Halloween with little Maggie was the adventure of my elementary school day.

Sincerely,

Johnny

THIRTEEN DAYS IN OCTOBER

During the President Kennedy inauguration speech, he said "fellow Americans, asked not what your country can do for you, instead asked what you could do for your country." He also challenged America to be the defended of the free world "to preserve democracy from tyrant and communisms."

I personally think his most famous speech was "let the torch be lilted, born on this day, a generation of Americans go forth to defend the freedom of the free worlds."

13 days in October was about the Cuban Missiles Crises. U-2 spy plane take photos of missiles sites around the nation of Cuba, information's forwarded to President Kennedy and his military advisers. A blockade or quarantined was to prevent the Soviet Unions from sending any military equipments toward Cuba. Kennedy gave an ordered to Premier Khrushchev to dismantle the nuclear missiles bases and shipped it back to Russia. For thirteen days either sides wished to give in. Temper, arguments from both sides was heated up.

U. S. made it clear, if any Russian Submarines resurfaced, their destroyer's will opened fire, telling them to return back. During the 7th or 8th days the blockade seems to be going well for America, when a Soviet Sub stop, didn't surfaced or challenged the U.S. Navy. U.S.S. Enterprise and U.S.S. Forrestal her aircraft's now armed with nuclear warhead was ready to strike, if Russians vessels challenged the U.S.

President Jack Kennedy finally appeared on live T.V. to address the issues to the American people concerning the crises. The nation was in full alert our armed forces declared a state of emergency, rising the conflict to decor -2, meaning a full thermo-nuclear conflict now existed between the people of the Soviet Unions and the people of the United States.

Tragedy struck on the eleven or 12ᵗʰ days, since one of our U-2 spy plane was shot down by a SAM, surface to air missile, Kennedy was in a very tough situation, should he waited for full confirmations' that Major Anderson aircraft was shot down, maybe he needed to give the green light for our military forces to invade Cuba. Kennedy gave Khrushchev 36 hours to respond, before the U. S. will strike.

The next day Premiere Khrushchev responded with a letter, stating the Soviet Unions will destroyed the nuclear bases her fleet will sailed back to Russia. To this day, it was terribly sad, Premiere Khrushchev did not received or given one percent of credit for his decision to with drawl the missiles from Cuba. He died without receiving any credits for his policy for peaceful co-existed with NATO and her allies. Had he never responded to Kennedy ordered or challenged the might of America, many millions of innocents lives will be dead on both sides.

Next day Kennedy speech, don't know the exact quote, something like this "man had the capabilities, responsibilities' to build weapons that could destroyed lives on Earth." "We must all come to a understanding many innocents lives could be destroyed, because of this atomic age." "We're all inhabited this Earth, in which we lived in, we must learned to share the abundant, the air we breathe, we're human and we're all immortal."

Sincerely,

Johnny Wong

WENDELL'S LOVE

Though out my life, I had pastors that came and go. Him and his wonderful wife came during the summer of 05'. There was something difference about him. I shared with Alan, Wendell never do anything fancies or super to reach, comfort others, yet is the small stuff, which amazed me the most.

Yes both me and him, even Julie agreed he was very stubborn at certain issues. Both, hard headed, disagreeing at certain moments, simpler banging each other head against the steel door. Yet, despite our arguing at some circumstances, there's a genius loving side to Wendell, a soft spoken heart inside of him.

Unlike to many Christians boosted about loving God. Well they mentioned talked is cheap, but with him, he demonstrated with actions. I recalled while working with a Chinese Computer Firm, where an elderly man took a piece of wood, threaded me to a physical confrontation, I told him I cursed at him. He showed his love toward me with compassion, explaining even though, I wrong him 10%, the elderly person was more at fault, because he wrong me 90%. Sad to say, my former supervisor questioned me, "why did you cursed at him." My pastor showed more loved by not asking me that question.

I remember one pastor told me to get my act together, when I said to him,"even though your words and actions hurt me, I wanted to forgive you and that God loves you. He was ignorant, arrogant kept on telling me not to leave, we had to talk about it." Yet the more he brought up the past, defending himself, it was hurting me every moments. In all the pastor, I knew Wendell never showed the self-righteous in him.

As I am finishing writing this letter, I thank Wendell, all those difficult times, he still encouraged me to never give up hope, in God. He still believed someday God will heal me of my illness. He spoke to me "Johnny, if you had to take your medicine last day on Earth, God had already performed a miracle in you."

My final message to Wendell, Julie, the rest of C.T. members, "Johnny gives a lot, demanded a lot, someday his the nicest guy on planet Earth, other days, his a very angry S. O.B." On the other hand he never lost his sense of humor. Since his in-law is Irish, common joke with the Irish, they fight best when their drunk."

Wendell, don't worried about responding, as long as you thank me in your heart, that will be enough.
As a favor keep this note in your wallet, someday when I am gone, that's how I wished you to remember our friendship.

Sincerely,

Johnny

A STORY ABOUT BABY TERESA

Not long ago today, if you're measured in time. A beautiful, little, cutie pie, darling, precious "Baby Teresa" was born. Her eye's must be very tired, the day, mommy and daddy brought her home from the hospital.

As" Baby Teresa" resting in the crib, our nations people hurting economically, due to high unemployment rate. Many people jealous of China economic success. The world looked pretty dark, violence hatreds racing across the globe, especially in the Middle East. School violence in America, Catholic Priest sandals. Penn State Foot Ball Team sad news.

In the area of sport, China for the first time, won more gold medals during the Summer Olympic in Beijing 2008. In the area of NBA Basketball Gemini Lin broke the color barrier, became the first Asian American with the New York Knick. In baseball Yankee's finally won the world series since the year 2000. In winter Olympic U.S. men hockey team lost a very closed game to the Canadians. The bright size women team took the precious beat the Canadians. Any team could upset Canada for the Gold, Chinese are cheap, but Johnny is never cheap with women. He didn't cared what nation could upset the Canadians', he' will take them out for a good Chinese dinner. To this day Canadians Consulates continued to denied him of citizenships.

All these bad, negative news, plus total darkness. A miracle before our eyes, today, not just any other day, indeed a special day. A day of hope, goodwill triumph, over evil, darkness. "Baby Teresa" was born. "Baby Teresa" a beautiful named, after "Mother Teresa." Her named challenged us to live in world to over come anger, revenged, hate, violence, but to installed love in one's heart. Her husband James, lovely wife Anna gave her this name, not just any ordinary name, but to represent "Baby Teresa," motherhood of man kind.

Someday as "Baby Teresa", grew older, she's symbolized the loved, comforting around the world marked by suffering, her amazing birth called for a world to understand, lived in harmory, extending compassionate to people who had never experiences joys, affections, yet we, including myself maybe having a hard time, forgiving, letting go of the past. "Baby Teresa" birth challenged us all not to give up on God, in the mist of difficult circumstances, there's where Chirst and God speaks to our heart.

Sincerely,

Johnny Wong

BEATLE'S FOR KELLY'S

Love me do.

Which is your favorite soup.

From me to you.

There' s a band called who.

I want to hold your hand.

Do know a girl named Fran?

All my loving.

Kelly is forgoing.

Can't buy me love.

Kelly an angel from above.

You got to hide your love away.

No monies for Kelly's hideaway.

We can work it out.

Being cheap with a girl, don't shout.

Norwegian Wood.

As a teenager, we're wished to be cool.

In my life.

Someday you're a beautiful wife.

Strawberry Field Forever.

Loosing weeper, founder, keeper.

Penny Lance.

Your baby be called Mary Jane.

St. Pepper's Lonely Hearts Club Band.

Berry grew on a piece of land.

Across the Universe.

On your birthday, shrimp fried rice.

For you're holy, you're precious, a song, a lyric, Beatle's forever on your Birthday. By Uncle Johnny

CHRISTAMS FOR EVA

Hark the Angel sings.

On a piano, notes A, B, C, abiding, brightly, center swing.

Angel we have heard on high.

Every boy does fine for your sight.

The First Noel.

Two whole step, equal Eva sleigh bell.

Do you Hear, what I Hear.

A symphony, D Major, dwelling, falling on dear.

The Little Drummer Boy.

C#, G#, Crying on Christ gentles, falling, for Roy.

Away in a Manger.

Whole Note, Half Note, equal a ranger.

God rest you Gentlemen.

G Major Chord, your gentle, boldness, sentiment.

Joy to the World.

Treble Clef, Bass Clef, striking each key, is round.

Rudolph the Ring Reindeer.

Middle C, Created Eva musketeer.

Silently Night, Holy Night.

Harmonic and Melodic interval, on a ride.

It's the most Wonderful Time of the year.

G Flats, A Flats, B Flats, equal Eva greatness,
attitude boast liked a star.

Christmas Time is Here.

7^{Th} and Octave equal Eva birthday is near.

Every Holiday, Thanksgiving, Christmas come and
go, but the wonderful relationship I had with Eva
will always remembered her in my heart.

Sincerely, Johnny Wong.

HANUKKAH FOR JULIE'S

Growing up as a little girl, Julie dream of helping people that was less fortunate than her.

During our session, I often asked "the meaning Hanukkah?" I never knew what was about, even to this day. She explained to me "it had to do with the city of Jerusalem." Julie "what is the meaning of lighting the seven candles?"

Out of all the counselors, I had she's was the best. That's time, wishing our sessions never ended. One thing I admired about her, if she's didn't agreed with me, she showed no anger never saw her rising her voice.

maybe to a Christian, very hard to understand. Who know Julie maybe some day, a very pretty Jewish girl asked me to marry her, then she's explained to me the full meaning of Hanukkah.

Julie dream came true on Hanukkah, when she got her clinical license social worker, also received a wonderful job with F. E. G. S. On this holiday, whatever religion we are, Jews, Christians, Muslims, Hindus, Moslems, Islam, Buddhists, let's put our differences aside, come have a seat. A banquet dinner, a seat of brothers and sisters, enjoyed the international cuisines.

On this Hanukkah, I choose to remember Julie, her love and personalities. She's had given so much in life. I owe her so much. Whenever I asked her, "how could I repaid her?" She often said "Johnny two words of thank you, will be fine."

I might not have a lot to said "about Julie", she always enjoyed reading my writing. It is always out of my heart in honor of writing in her name. On this Hanukkah that's how I choose to remember Julie Magaril.

Sincerely,

Johnny Wong

MR. CASEY SENIOR

I had never meet Gerry dad's. He told me "Johnny Wong, if he was alive today, you're really liked him." How do you write to a person, which is no longer around and never knew this person? I guessed since the holiday season approached, by me of writing to him, that's how I keep his memories alive.

Gerry explained to me "working in the coal mine, the hours was long, very dirties." "The danger of cave-in where many coal miners was trapped, they're die of lack of oxygen." I am pretty sure his dad witnessed some of his friend's perished from cave-in. Lucky Mr. Casey Senior never experiences it.

None of us were born with a sliver spoon in our month. Similar to my parents, we're all have it hard. I guessed Mrs. Casey Senior also took odd jobs to support Gerry and John. Many coal miners die around 50-60 years of age, because of Black Lung.

In the state Pennsylvanian, there wasn't a whole lot of opportunities, especially for girls, women. Most of them were waitresses, sale clerk, working in department store as cashiers, if they were very lucky, not a whole lot some became teachers, employed in the hospital as nurses or librarians.

For men they're many followed their dad's footstep by employing in the coal mine. Even in the cities of Pittsburg, Allen Town, didn't had the opportunities liked New York, even in the city of Philly, many individuals commuted to Manhattan NYC for jobs. From Philly to NY only about two hours trip.

Since, I never had a good relationship with my dad, so many occasions, wished I could shake Mr. Casey Senior, give him a hug and said "I am pleased to meet you." "Your son Gerry mentioned you're a great person." On this Christmas by writing to those who wasn't around that's how we keep that individuals, their spirits alive. Yet I was so happy to get a chance, having a great moment with Mrs. Casey Senior.

If his dad was alive today, he'll be very happy see his son married to a very pretty Chinese girl. I still remembered some of things said by the priest during the sermon "Cindy first love was helping people, nursing was her talent, when it came to assisting the patients, she was best in what she did." "If Gerry did not kissed Cindy on the lip, then she'll turned to stone." "Now to the audiences, pleased Johnny didn't said this. It was the Priest, who were conducting their marriage."

Thank you Gerry for giving me the time to keep your dad spirits alive. Happy New Year, have splendid day at work.

Sincerely,

Johnny Wong

RIVER OF LOVE

Heroes are never born, but created in the image of God.

On that historic day of June 84', a very sweet,
lovely, woman kindly greeted me.

That special person none other than Mary Williams. Our wonderful friendship grew as the current of a mighty river. Her love for person, her unique personalities, similar to the flow as the honey comb.

A flesh spring of lovely water over flowing the river bank. Unlike any other river, Mary Williams river consisted of Irish Spring, melting with a taste of honey sugar.

That similar act of kindness symbolized touching, wonderful relationship which still communicated in words also through payer.

Mary's love in a river running smoothly down the path of my live. Her river flowed as her generosity, a relationship of an Italian Chef.

Her river is a life of flowing energy, an expression of smiled, love for a world, especially suffering little children's.

Mary she's had also suffered greatly in life, yet out of kindness, she's still found ways to comfort people.

None of us really understood the meaning of live, usually, including myself how come, bad things happened to good people.

My friend in Greece said "John do not blame God for the suffering, because men and women choose to live a sinful life, they continued to act in evil, wicked things. Though out decades, including centuries, God waited for men and women to repent from their wicked ways.

I admired and desired Mary expression, how she's often opened up her house, inviting me for a cup of tea and dinner many occasion.

I could made million of monies, achieved fame by my writing, but that's no greater joy, than Mary holding on to me, that's no greater joy than falling into the arms of Mary Williams.

My last day on Earth, I'll still take out my pen and write something for Mary.

HAPPY BIRTHDAY MARY ! ! ! !
Sincerely,
Johnny Wong

When suffering, also compassion

About three weeks ago, I saw a movie entitled "Raid on Entebbe." In July 1976 Palestinians hijacked an "Air France" airline on its route from Athens Greece to France.

Security was terrible, so the plane was hijacked quickly. Their final destination was Uganda Africa. President of Uganda and several terrorists joined the remaining forces. The President and Palestinians dangerous mistakes was letting the non-Jewish passengers released.

The non-Jews told the "Israeli arm forces, how many terrorists, Ugandan soldiers, also information surrounding. This vital information given to the Israel government.

President extended the deadline to July 4, midnight. Jewish soldiers stormed the old terminal where the hostages were staying. In a cross fire between the Israelis and the terrorists, a Jewish hostage, turned his back, saw the leader of the terrorist about to pull the pin of a hand grenade, they both stared at each other.

Finally second, he placed the hand grenade on top of the counter of the table. Knew he was going to be killed by the commandoes, he fought it out with them and die.

To this day, I don't know all the facts, details, maybe this incident did occurred between these two men. Yet in the moment this terrorist showed a lot of love, compassion and understanding in his own heart. Most likely, he maybe felt a lot of guilt, condemnation, if he ever pulled the pin and tossed their hand grenade toward those innocent hostages'.

I guessed in times of our killing, suffering, hatreds, against the human race, there's compassions within our enemies.

Shakespeare once mentioned "A Quality of Mercy is liked the drop of rains, blessing among us, yet in the mist of suffering, we could also extended a quality of mercy for our enemies."

Sincerely

Johnny Wong

MRS. CASEY SENIOR

How do I remembered Gerry mom's Mrs. Casey Senior? As I am writing this story, I think about 12 years when I first meet at Logan International Airport in Boston. As I was waiting at the airport arrival area, noticed a pretty White elderly blonde haired woman sitting down. I approached her and said "are you Mrs. Casey, Gerry mom's." "Why yes who are you?" She asked. I am Cindy younger brother named Jack. "Well I am very pleased to meet you."

"I am waiting for Gerry to pick us up to Cape Cod." "Yeah me too." She's responded. I knew that point on, I was going to struck oil, a gold mine, not in terms material needs, but a wonderful friendship with Mrs. Casey Senior. "My son Gerry not very good in keeping his appointment, usually not on time." "Ah don't worry is not only Gerry none of us are, sometime including myself arriving on time."

From the bottom of my heart, those time with her, holding her hand, going by the lake, picking Blue Berries, going to mass., kissing her on the cheek. Those were special times, moments, that I had with Gerry mom's.

No monies, materials needs, possessions, could replaced Mrs. Casey Senior. That was my very first time, in Cape Cod, it was to be my last, yet my finest hours in the state Massachusetts. There's no greater joy than sitting next to her, holding Gerry mom hand, going to the beach with.

She's was full of joy holding, carrying Nicole, to her to mass., church on Sunday morning. Smiling, playing with Nicole.

Today we lived in a world of technology, with cell, phones, emails, computers, people driving fancy cars liked BMW, Mercedes Ben, Honda Sport cars, none of this could replaced the joyous moments, the love, the human kindness, genteelness, sweetness, compassions, understanding the human heart of Mrs. Casey Senior.

Live is very short, we don't have a whole a lot of time, anything could happened to us, we might be gone at any period, yet we must share and remembered those special moments, we must work things, together. There's a Beatle's song, entitled "We can work things out."

As I am writing this letter, I might not be considered Gerry mom, any blood or closed relatives, my grandmother Go Poor pass away of weeks ago, but she's live to be 102, or 103.

Today Gerry I considered Mrs. Casey Senior part of my family and today she's my grandmother, that's how I choose to remembered the love of Mrs. Casey Senior.

Thank you Gerry, thank you for letting me write this letter, drive carefully, have a great day at work.

Sincerely

Johnny Wong

CHRISTMAS IS

Christmas is a time of giving and receiving. With the latest school shooting. How do we defined the happiest season of the year. During this time, also high suicides rate. Christmas could also be depressed, especially to those whose family members pass away.

In this hour of difficult times, we often asked ourselves "God despite all this hard situation, do you care, you're so far away?" In our suffering we, including myself "asked God where are you?"

I told my niece Nicole and Kelly Casey "Your Uncle didn't really live a good, righteous, holy live, he done a lot bad and evil deeds himself." I'll never wanted you followed Uncle Johnny footstep." "I always wanted what's best for you and Kelly."

Since I have a mental conditions, tried not to use it as an excused for my actions. Wendell sermon was correct "if we think what this world can offer us, than we're missing a bigger picture what Heaven is in store for us."

God is in control of all circumstances and in all situations our God reign. I don't care how many bad things a person did in he or her life, I tried to reach out, encouraged and prayed for that individual.

Some of us, might not received a whole lot of things for Christmas, well nobody said "life was fair." Let's us rejoiced on this day our savior Jesus Christ was born and on Good Friday, he died on the cross for our sins.

My only advice how matter how hard you're suffering is, never give up on God, he is our only hope in life.

Wendell and Julie pleased take my writing for is for you.

Sincerely,

Johnny

ODE TO ESTHER

Look into your eyes and I see a paradise forming. I see trees, lakes, water flowers and birds signing in the air. I saw you swimming in the water in that golden swimsuit. Who else can swim in the crystal blue water? Who can guide your body through the water gracefully?

It is none other than Esther Williams. At that time, she was the fastest swimmer on Earth. You were training for the Olympic when World War 11 begin. You used to model bathing suit in department store.

When you put on that suit, transformed into a beautiful woman, lot of actor admired your pretty figure. You were like a fish out of water, swam like a human torpedo, moving body under water, you are like a submarine. As you came up for air you're appeared like a swan duck.

As years go by, Hollywood came knocking at your door. They haunted you down and captured you. From now Esther became a movie star. First film debut in 1944 and the rest became history.

You swam like a mermaid. When you are near me, I feel your heart beat, I can listen to you breathing in my ear, and see your beautiful figure traveling like a luxury liner in the water, feet kicking, pictured Hollywood leading men dancing, swimming, under water with you.

Whenever put on that swimsuit, there's magic flowing within your body. When you were in water, it obeyed your command. You dressed like a shining armor. As years passed by you swam with Hollywood leading men. Then in 1955, made last swimming movie with MGM, you hung up your suit, the water slowly disappeared when you retired. There will be no other swimmer that will bear your name.

Lyrics taken from Jefferson Star ships "Nothing Going to Stop Us Now."

Lyrics taken from the song "Groovy Kind of Love."

A GENTLE GIANT

Yesterday I heard about the Simon and Linda dad's. I was a little shocked by the news. I recalled a couple years ago, we struck an interesting conversation, in regard to the economic, board of directors, corporations, federal reserved, chief executive, officials. Less not forget I too was a business major at Queens Borough Community College.

Right now I don't what to say. I might not be very close to him. By writing to Mr. Wong Senior, could imaged him sitting, next to me. Writing about him keep his spirits alive. It is similar a of flaming fire, being lilted by a torch. The flaming torch, symbolic his greatness, kindness, compassions, understandings, gentleness of his personalities.

In all his way, he remained liked a gentleman, if he didn't disagreed with you, never screamed, raised his voice at anybody. As looked back those years, there was loving side to him. His loved for my nieces', nephews', let's not forget Amanda and Christina.

Like most Chinese immigrates that arrived to this country, most Chinese family, didn't struck oils, diamonds' or a gold mines. We live in tenement housing, even Dr. Casey family's didn't have all that easy.
If our parents didn't made, they sacrificed, desiring our kids, could enjoyed the luxuries' Simon, Linda her brother, Reggie, Amanda and Christina also.

I was always proud Mr. Wong Senior of his accomplishments in employee of a bank. Back in his days, not a whole Chinese work for an American Bank and there wasn't too many Asians bank's. I might not accomplished a whole in life, at the same time, if my writing could reached out and comfort others, that's what writing all about.

I wished I could see him one more time. The conversation, I mentioned earlier it was to be our final, yet, considered the best dialogued we both enjoyed. Well I ran out ideas. In Simon, Linda, my family, the Casey, Wade his brother, his wife Christian and Reggie, in our heart, Mr. Wong Senior personalize the cool, gentleman. Today let's us remembered him as a gentle giant.

Sincerely,

Johnny Wong

A STORY ABOUT MY GRANDMOTHER

Our grandmother's was a kind, gentle, compassion and generous person. When we first arrived to America, our grandmother, grandfather probably the first to see.

Grand mom, what we admired her was her sense of humor. It was never about her, whatever she's had, it was usually for the family. Grand mom could be angry at times, on the other hand, out of her love, she never held any resentment toward anybody.

I remembered as a little kid, once she's took me to China Town for bowl of Noodles. I recalled during my stay at the Laundry Mat, normally came cooked Chicken Wings for Lunch. Out of her heart, she's sacrificed by eating the skin of the bones, so me and sister could enjoyed our meal.

How she's lived her life, is never about her, her life center around our family. Her love for little kids, just overwhelmed me most of the time.

We're proud to have a grandmother who never took life for granted, who always showed gratitude. Our grandmother lived a long life full of happiness, and love. I am happy, we're all proud for our grandmother. I don't have a whole lot to say, yet this is how I remembered grand mom.

Sincerely,

Johnny Wong

COMMENCEMENT ADDRESS FOR NICOLE

Unlike any other day, today you're special in the heart, mind, soul of the Wong's and Casey's clans. On this graduation day, the warm sun shined a patch, skies opened up, showers of blessing falling upon you.

Imaged writing a diary, each pages embank life of Nicole Casey. First page, December 12, 1991, birth of Nicky. She was the first baby to arrive within the Wong's and Casey's families'. "Uncles, aunts, grandparents waiting to put their arms' around, carrying, playing with you.

Each page, similar to romantic novel. First birthday day enjoyable occasion at a Thai restaurant. Friends, peoples, relatives, laughing, smiling, until their teeth fell out, drinking liked drunkard Irish. Common jokes, the Irish fights best when their drunk's.

Being Baptism, little babies over the whole, a sound of crying in endless joy. A joy of little kids running in the playground. Every girl loved to charm. Nicky, extended a cry of pleasant.

As she's grown older entered elementary school. Loveable Mrs. Redman adored her, if tomorrow never end. Her pet teacher, in an imagery mother figure toward Nicole. Mrs. Redman inspired her to reach, loved, care, showed, compassion toward individuals who were less fortunate than her.

At the middle of her diary entered into junior high. A time of adolescent, times day dream about boys, a times for her to gather with her friends. Playing the violin to the tune of "Chariots of Fires." Also "My Heart will go on." Her beautiful simile rhymed multiplies by melody over flowing sweet honey, divided Nicole charming loved of endless suffering children's in world where the haves and haves not. Her loved, understanding, compassion, sweet than the honey, more desired than much fine gold.

Going from pages to pages, her life takes us to a sparking journey, as she's graduated from Saints Francis De Salle. She's blossomed into a beautiful princess. Finally entered in a Catholic girls school, Dominican Academy, here's in a place where girls matured into woman hood.

Similar to JFK speech "asked not what this country can do for you, instead asked what you can do for your country." Nicky took the called of Kennedy inauguration by responding taking a class trip to a third world country called Ecuador, she's lived with the poor. Demonstrated people who have little in a world, some how showed more gratitude than people who had more possessions in this universe.

Her graduation signify at Dominican Academy Nicole was going to do greatness toward mankind, plus women also. Similar to Neil Armstrong "One small leap, one giant step for Mankind." Similar to "Uncle Johnny" is never about Nicole, is the people who influenced her from the time when she's a little baby to full woman hood.

Today the final chapter of her diary, as they announced Nicole Tai Way Casey, as she's picked up her degree. "Uncle John, Aunt Joe, Momma Linda, Jim, Mary Megan, Wai, Reggie, Kelly, her God parents, sister Kelly, brother Sean, Uncle Simon, Aunt Linda, Aunt Suzy, Aunt Margaret, Christina, Armada, grandparents wanted to say

"CONGRATULATION NICOLE CASEY AND TO THE CLASS OF 2013 ! ! !

Dear Nicky the apostle Peter gave you the key to unlocked the future of this world, go enjoyed the taste, live, breath, the goodness of live, most importance lived life to the fullest.

Ideas taken from JFK inauguration speech and astronaut Neil Amstrong.

Love Always, Uncle Johnny.
Lyrics taken from Christian hyme Pslam 19.

COMMENCEMENT FOR KELLY

With the advancement of computers, cell phones, electronic components, our universe in which we lived seems to get smaller and smaller. Unlike the day's of Columbus, people back then tend to enjoyed lives better. Time traveled diminished the world in a rapidly fast pace.

Kelly's birth brought changed in world marked by hates, and violence. Kelly a beautiful Irish named for a very cute baby. Her birth symbolized the hoped, loved, compassions for the Irish peoples. 1996 a cease fire between the Irish Republican Armies and The Royal British Armies in Belfast Northern Ireland.

Her world centered the loved of little children's, not just physical pain, also assisting emotional, hunger of those whose' less fortunate than her. Her compassions, understanding loved for humanities marked a turning point, to challenged people of all races, ethnics, religions, gender, physical, emotional, never give up on God. In this world there's all we have.

January 29, 1996, a year in milestone, little, cute, chubby, round face baby Kelly came into our lives, also brought a finally lasting peace for her people the Catholic Irish Community. Peace finally arrived at the heart of Belfast Northern Ireland.

Out of all my nieces, she's still is one of the cutest, funniest, laughing. No greater joy, than holding her, babysitting, buying her ice creams, ices, helping her riding a two wheel bicycle when she's four years old, carrying her to the beach, brining her to school, seeing beloved teacher Mrs. Redman smiling.

Greatest accomplishments out of 9,000 applicants, she's auditions' singing a Civil War Song "Shenandoah" to get into "LaGuardia Performing Arts." Lived your dream, don't sell short, aimed for the stars. I had you confidences in you to attend as much theater plays, see more entertaining movies as possible.

Your times has come, today parents, aunts, uncles, brothers, sisters, relatives, mom, dad, God parents and the Megan, all very exciting seeing you in a beautiful pink green dress walking toward the podium to see you crying as you received your high school diploma.

If "Uncle Johnny" could write you a lyric, a song for a beautiful princess. May a song written for Kelly for her loved for the endless suffering children's who never knew loved in their heart, to those hungry kids going to bed without foods.

Let her sing an anthem, piano playing, finger touching the sound of a new generations. May lyrics as imagery, creativity, poetic as Lennon and Mc Carty. Piano playing added by melody, in additions to harmony, multiply by the beauty of Kelly's beautiful lovely voice echoed to the sound rhyming to the beat of a difference drum.

Go enjoyed life, lived life to the fullest. Pleased do not be discouraged, be willingly to accept criticism. Live big, dream big. On a clear summer night, looked up toward the sky, every stars represented an actress named, their achievement. Every star shined as brightly in a clear beautiful summer night. Someday your name will be counted in the heavenly skies above Bell Harbor.

CONGRATULATION ! ! ! KELLY AND TO THE CLASS OF 2013.

Sincerely,

Uncle Johnny

PASSION FOR WRITING

About two or three years ago, my friend Tony said "in his architect class, the professor mentioned I knew most of you have talent, but if you couldn't handle criticisms, then you don't belong to this classes." That goes for writing also.

Me and brother Simon are very stubborn, both pretty angry, similar hitting our head into brick wall. On Christmas night he criticisms my piano playing, nothing big, just a humor joke. Got so upset, tried to avoid him. Yet he did showed me a lot loved. Later on needed to apologize to him. From that day on, I learned to sorrow my pride. I could be rejected by a hundred or maybe more from publishers and editors. They're said "Mr. Wong we enjoyed reading your manuscripts', unfortunately we cannot published your work, we found some people who are more qualify than you."

First of all, a writer should never be arrogant, having the macho imaged, oh I am going to be successful, made a lot monies, all those girls waiting for my autographs. That's not a writer, he or she must be humble, not having high expectations, had to lower his expectations. If any author only think's about monies and success, than a waste of my time typing out this letters.

The definitions of passion for writing, writing is emitted in my blood. I do it, because I enjoyed it. When I write, I felt the force similar to "Star War" I felt the force flowing within my hands. My writing is never about me. Elisa gave me the greatest gift, a person could possessed. Is never about me, my writing is about individuals, who influence me from childhood adulthood. An author who only mentioned about himself, to me not a very good writers. Nobody desired to hear his boring story. What determined a good writer he writes about other people.

Yes is importance to have good grammars and spellings. On the other hand there are many good writers, grammars, spelling prevent them to be a good writers. Back during my high school days, there was no things such as creative writing, instead they're teach you about Shakespeare, nothing wrong about, but when we're grew up, nobody going to talk like him. My philosophy is if you cannot sit down and write for two to three hours straight, then you're fit to be called a writer.

Passion for writing looked at it as a way to reach out, comforted others who's going through difficulties periods in their life. The key to any writing is imagery, creativity, poetic. Those are the success in becoming a good writers. My final conclusions that's what's passion for writing all about.

Sincerely

Johnny Wong

December 7,1991

USS ARIZONA MAJESTIC FLAGSHIP LIVES FOREVER

On the morning of the 19th of June 1915 the birth of a new battleship came forth out of the Brooklyn Navy Yard in New York. On this historic day she was proudly commissioned into the United States Navy. She was the third ship in the U.S. Navy to bear the name of her state. She was called the USS Arizona.

From this day on she begin her precious voyage by sailing the mighty sea of the two oceans. She's the flagships of the battle force of the Atlantic Fleet, then switched over to the Pacific Fleet in 1921. In 1930's participated on numerous war games. Her architectural design a flashing beauty to be viewed at. Arizona the most powerful ship to travel across the vast beautiful ocean of the Pacific.

Even though she had never opened fired with her big guns on the enemies, the sight of her 14inch gun turret frighten any warship that crossed her path. No ship would dare to challenge her mighty fire power from her cannons.

Then on that fateful morning of 7th of December day something happened to you. Early dawn, Sunday, men were quickly asleep aboard your ship. While the harbor and our nation was resting peacefully, the enemy slowly creep, secretly sneaked in to surprise us. The enemy had awaken us. Then suddenly the unexpected happened. Like a mighty earth quake destruction had upon you. You blew up liked a volcano. There we left you crying for help. Your cried for help sounded liked thunder. Unfortunately we wanted to help you so badly, but our country was caught unprepared.

All this precious time we could prevented you from this terrible tragedy, instead we were resting heavily all alone. Death had took you away liked a thief in the night. The beloved people of Arizona will never see you fight again. Death had taken you away from this nation.

Oh rise majestic Arizona flagship battleship, will fight on for another day. We are one nation that will fight in your honor. We had avenged your death by crippling the enemy fleet in Midway, Guadalcanal, Solomon Islands, New Guinea, Marshall Islands Turk Lagoon Guam, liberation of the Philippines, Okinawa to the surrendered of the Japanese's militaries in Tokyo Bay aboard the USS Missouri, the Allies engaged revenged of your death by wining the war both in Europe and in the Pacific.

Today is your 50th year universities, even though you're at the bottom of the harbor, the whole nation morn over you. To this very day, you still communicated to us by sending little gases of bubble up to the surface of the sea. Sleep tight, rest gentle, may you and your gallant men rest in peace for ever. You had never opened fire on the enemy, you had never been in action, but on that fateful morning of 7th of December you done the best, anybody could called for. Our country will never fall asleep again. We will stand by to protect and guard tilt eternity. There will be no other ship liked you or to bear your name.

Sincerely,

Johnny Wong

Princess Mermaid

Could you danced to Fred Astaire?

A ballerina swim to Swan Lake.

A mermaid swim in prefect pair.

Katie monies or gold I do not possessed.

Imagined a mermaid named on a cheesecake.

Esther Williams, Eleanor Holmes, Gail Johnson, impressed.

Tracy Rudi, Carol Waldo, Christina Jones performed to seaquake

Ballerina, plus gymnastic, multiply, moment, divided a synchronized tale.

Katie love, in addition, goodness, multiply compassion, a swimmer wale.

A mermaid swim to the tune on a keyboard.

Note c, her caring, e notes electrify, f notes, folly, Gershwin.

A guitar fingerboard, A major chord, exciting, audio, for Katie a castle.

Sherbet, Mozart, Bach, Beethoven, a mermaid tail fin.

Joyful, joyful we adore thee, a mermaid arrived a parcel.

Starry, Starry night, tale of a Princess Mermaid desired.

More desired than fine gold sweeter than the Honeybees.

A trumpet, flute, sting quartet, a mermaid rehearsal.

A guitar, piano, synthesizer, a synchronizer swimmer dance, swim to "Chariot of Fire."

A violin, bass, cello, melody for Santa Carla Aquarium.

Amy Grant, Phil Keaggy, Keith Green, Larry Norman, a synchronized sapphire.

Sing your praise to the lord, your swimming, dancing honorarium.

El Shaddai, a lyric, a song for Katie Sapada.

Beatles for forever, we can work it out.

Bryan Adams summer of 69' Santa Carla armada.

In my life, a symphony, blessing of rain drop.

For I do not known Katie, thinks she's very sweet, wonderful Christian. Only favor if you could win the gold for me in the 2016 Olympic. Sincerely, Johnny Wong

CHINESE FOOD MR. RATHE

Early dawn Chinese Dim Sum at your doorstep.

Egg Roll, Finger Roll, Shrimp Roll followed your footstep.

Wanton Soup, Sweet and Sour Soup served at convenient.

Chicken Fried Rice, Pork Fried Rice, Shrimp Fried Rice, obedient.

Beef Chow Fun, Beef Lo Mei, Beef with Pepper.

Shrimp Lo Mei, Chicken Lo Mei, Beef Lo Mei, don't get hyper.

Pei King Duck, Roast Duck, let's celebrated.

Sweet Sour Pork, Sweet Sour Chicken on a platter.

Combination Platter arrival earlier.

Mix Vegetable, Mix Chickens, Vegetable with rice, rapidly.

Chinese Pastries, can not completed with France.

Iron Chef battle Chinese cuisine considered a trance.

Non-Chinese Women must have Chinese food, or less cannot survived.

Pork Bund, Hot Dog Bund, Siemens Bund, Coconut, Pineapple Bund advice.

Chicken Wings, Chicken Breast, Chicken Leg, never always.

Egg Custards, Sweet Ice Tea, Honey Comb Drink on a summer afternoon.

Chicken Chow Mei, Chicken Chop Surry, for early Chinese immigrant.

Egg Roll Cookies, Coconut Cookies, Strawberry, Lime, Cookies.

Friendships, with Doral's round as Golden Fleece.

Mango Milk Shakes, Strawberry Milk Shakes, Leeches Drinks.

Red Bean Drink, Sweet Milk Drink, Pineapples Drinks, brink.

There's something about international cuisine, in a world marked by violence, non-sensed anger, hatred,

Why don't we all sit down as human being, let's shared an international cuisine with all people of difference

Colors, gender, rich or poor, religions, let's enjoyed a wonderful meal together.

Sincerely,

Johnny Wong

CHINESE FOOD FOR DORL'A

Early dawn Chinese Dim Sum at your doorstep.

Egg Roll, Finger Roll, Shrimp Roll followed your footstep.

Wanton Soup, Sweet and Sour Soup served at convenient.

Chicken Fried Rice, Pork Fried Rice, Shrimp Fried Rice, obedient.

Beef Chow Fun, Beef Lo Mei, Beef with Pepper.

Shrimp Lo Mei, Chicken Lo Mei, Beef Lo Mei, don't get hyper.

Pei King Duck, Roast Duck, let's celebrated.

Sweet Sour Pork, Sweet Sour Chicken on a platter.

Combination Platter arrival earlier.

Mix Vegetable, Mix Chickens, Vegetable with rice, rapidly.

Chinese Pastries, can not completed with France.

Iron Chef battle Chinese cuisine considered a trance.

Non-Chinese Women must have Chinese food, or less cannot survived.

Pork Bund, Hot Dog Bund, Siemens Bund, Coconut, Pineapple Bund advice.

Chicken Wings, Chicken Breast, Chicken Leg, never always.

Egg Custards, Sweet Ice Tea, Honey Comb Drink on a summer afternoon.

Chicken Chow Mei, Chicken Chop Surry, for early Chinese immigrant.

Egg Roll Cookies, Coconut Cookies, Strawberry, Lime, Cookies.

Friendships, with Doral's round as Golden Fleece.

Mango Milk Shakes, Strawberry Milk Shakes, Leeches Drinks.

Red Bean Drink, Sweet Milk Drink, Pineapples Drinks, brink.

There's something about international cuisine, in a world marked by violence, non-sensed anger, hatred,

Why don't we all sit down as human being, let's shared an international cuisine with all people of difference

Colors, gender, rich or poor, religions, let's enjoyed a wonderful meal together.

Sincerely,

Johnny Wong

CHINESE NEW YEAR FOR JULIE

Being Chinese and Jew, we always have something in common. Now Julie pleased tried your best not to get angry about this statement. Common joke concerning Chinese and Jew, why do they're love each other so much, because they both worshiped monies.

Julie Chinese New Year not only Johnny New Year, is also your New Year too. The reason she's my best therapy. That day she's announced, "they going to put her in administrative duties." I was so hurt and disappointed.
She's very profession, if angry never raised her voice or used bad languages.

Being Jew and Chinese, both inherited common things on Earth. Our histories dated back thousands of years ago. Possessing an unique culture. Strived the importance of educations, in mathematics, sciences, every Jew loved Chinese food. In the area of physics, higher educations a great achievements. We loved classical music's, piano, guitars' considered the best.

Julie is never about me, I enjoyed writing people that influenced my life. In this world where so much violence, angers and hatreds, Julie gave me an excellent advice, trying to change people heart, will only hurt us, meaning high expectation on others.

She's taught me to accepted individuals of who, they're not based on the person skin colors. Additions with Joy, divided by love, subtracted by anger, multiplied her kindness, gentleness = Julie, compassion and understanding.

On this New Year, not only Johnny New Year, also Julie New Year, plus Dr. Weinstein, Andrew, Eva Goldstein, the receptionist by the front desk. Those three, four years, were specials and precious, I had with her.

Not only my holiday, Julie holiday also. Today give back something for Julie.

Sincerely

Johnny Wong

A MOTHER FIGURE

Now a day with the emotions, plus the rejections of Caucasians Women, my anger just kept on adding more fuel, gasoline ready to erupted similar to a violent volcano. At the same time, I asked my counselor "why m y anger and hatred turned into fear." "Johnny you don't wanted to get rejected again by this group of women."

Sometime glancing at a pretty brunette woman walking on the street. My mind often traveled back toward my fifth grade elementary school teacher Mrs. Linda Zadan. Sometime the anger letters, seeking justice, demanding White Anglo Christian Women to understand the pain of a Chinese man.

One brother told me, "importance to seek justice, the Bible mentioned a lot about justice." I totally disagreed with his statement, because if a person always demanded being treated fairly', you're also desiring people to pity, feel sorry for you. On the other hand the book of John focused mainly about love especially 1John the word love, appeared about 20 times.

Yes, it would be nice, if all those White Women rejected me to go on public T.V. to said "I am sorry, could you pleased forgive me." Not easy, don't have the feeling to say this, "first of all, it was so long ago, even if they're ever read this article those women couldn't cared less, because I am the only one suffering not them.

Yet if I ever raped, done any violence toward this group of women. The one person who would really hurt is Linda Zadan. At moment I couldn't go to bed, not even having dinner, all I could think about demanding justice, seeking vengeance against them.

Why do some folks have more than others, while most children go to bed hungry. In the future, if my feeling or anger go out of control, the first person to pop up in my mind will be Mrs. Zadan. I am ashamed to admit, around that time, I had a crushed on her. I had not have any teacher as pretty, beautiful and gorgeous as Mrs. Zadan. She's also beautiful in her heart. One day, she's announced "whoever was good for one to two minutes, I'll give that person a picture of Mars." I knew I was going to get it, that's no way she was standing next to my desk.

I also think Mrs. Zadan, had some affections for me, but she's guard herself. The life she's gave to me, could never be replaced.

Sincerely

Johnny Wong

A GIANTIC HEART

I made a deal with you, if Gerry could convinced you to stay for dinner, I'll write something for you. Given the amount of time, the goodness you showed toward my nieces and nephews.

I never knew when I first meet him. Whenever our family came out to Belle Harbor, his generous heart overflowed liked an ice cream sundae, melted on marsh marrows, crumbed, with sweet butters on a hot summer day.

Bernie gentle heart on fire, loved for people, set a good example. Is not the big things that counts, smallest, gracious human kindness that he spoke. His never fancy, not boastful, not showing any pride, but his humble heart's. Once they spoke of the great Ted Williams, was the last player to bat. 400, his vision's was so great, he could viewed the out field, while he was battling.

In some way Bernie remained us of Ted Williams. He had a huge heart of giving to the less fortunates. His generosities, similar to Ted Williams, opening arms, showing loves, compassions, understanding, he carried the weight of this world.

I knew, he lost a lot in life, but never, giving in self-pities, feeling sorry for himself, instead he got out of the rocking chair and often assisted whoever needed help during "Hurricane Sandy." I was very hurt, very sad, as his dinner caught on fire, Cindy told me "he was using his water hole to put out the fire." I really wished, could shared a tear for Bernie.

Despite what he lost, out of the goodness of his heart, he came, provided care for my family's. My friend in Boston said "Johnny there are many selfish people in this world, they won't do anything unless, they're get something in returned." Many born again Christians or Charismatic Christians similar.

Yes before we could help others, we must meet our own first. We lived in an in perfect world, despite our suffering, must also learned to extend grace toward others. Talk is very cheap, if couldn't back it up with actions. Bernie demonstrated his loved and actions toward others.

Heroes are never born, but created in the image of God. Tonight kind of special, I finally got to see this wonderful, kind hearted person face to face, yet during that short period of time, his heart spoke out to us, when sufferings, that's also compassions. His not only my heroes, our heroes for those still suffering during "Hurricane Sandy." Tonight in my heart, Bernie is my heroes.

Sincerely,

Johnny Wong

THE MUNICH OLYMPIC

On clear cool September Day 1972, Summer Olympic being held once again on German soil. As the Israeli athletics entered the Olympic stadium, the Germans audiences gave a loud round of applause, yes maybe a standing ovations. Little know, the clapping, screaming and applause would turned into darkness, endless, innocents killing of eleven Israelis athletics, to this very day known as the" Munich Massacred."

Strange our family had moved into Queens on January 1972. This Olympic, a little surprised, for the very first time, being lived by a satellite. It was my final years of elementary school. As the announcer Jim McKay said the "West German Government gave to the nation of Israel, a couple of hundred millions dollars for the killing of six millions Jews." Even back then being twelve years old, I said "it doesn't really matter when innocents lives were taken, no matter how many monies, jewels, gold, jade will never bring back those precious lives."

Securities around the athletics compound were very poor. People didn't really needed to show their I.D. Also they're could grabbed whatever key to opened the rooms. Later some people saw men climbing over the fence with huge bag. One person remained himself, why men jumping over the fence with large bag, this is the second week of the Olympic. Most events were over, only major events were the track and field.

The next day Palestinians terrorists called themselves "The Black September." Entered into one of the Israeli athletic room, they were awakened, one of them a heavy weight lifter using all his strength, to sacrificed, so the other athletics' could escaped to freedom. Unfortunately two murdered in cold blood.

German authorities and the Jewish Prime Ministry tried real hard to make a deal, with the terrorists, instead they insisted Israeli government to released a certain numbers of terrorists from Israel jail, or less, if their demand was not meet, each athletic will be killed. Golden Meir final gambled, if her government issued passports to all the terrorists, entered into any countries, lives will be spared. They did not fall for it, instead the leader of the group, insisted a flight to the airport.

As German police about to storm into the compound to rescued the athletics, unfortunately it was too late, they're bound in chains, buses headed toward the Munich Airport. German commodores, military soldiers waiting to ambushed the "Black September Group." Sniper or sharp shooter place around the terminals to meet the threat.

Once the leader found out no pilot aboard the plane, they decided to kill all the hostages, also to fight it out with the commodores. It was one of the most horrible sight I ever witness, in one of the movies, one terrorist opened the helicopter door, threw a hand grenade, killing all the hostages, including two German pilots. The next thing one terrorist took a submachine gun killing all the hostages in the helicopter.

I was very anger to hear one of the sharp shooter missed their fire, later on I took it back, my statement, found out they're won't very well equipped without night scope. It didn't matter if the snipers had night scope, the ordeal happed happened so quickly, nothing very little could be done. I gave the German Government and the Israeli Government for not giving in to the demand of the terrorists.

Why do I write about this article, two mouths ago with the Boston Marathon Bombing, also go back to one day in September. My opinion every who wished to come into this country, are entitled to the American Dream. For those who desired a better future for their children's, by all means allowed into this country.

A Beatles song called "Revolution." The lyrics mention "if you talked about hate and destruction, brother you could counted me out." My message is the same thing with the Beatles lyrics.

also to fight it out with the commodores. It was one of the most horrible sight I ever witness, in one of the movies, one terrorist opened the helicopter door, threw a hand grenade, killing all the hostages, including two German pilots. The next thing one terrorist took a submachine gun killing all the hostages in the helicopter.

I was very anger to hear one of the sharp shooter missed their fire, later on I took it back, my statement, found out they're won't very well equipped without night scope. It didn't matter if the snipers had night scope, the ordeal happed happened so quickly, nothing very little could be done. I gave the German Government and the Israeli Government for not giving in to the demand of the terrorists.

Why do I write about this article, two mouths ago with the Boston Marathon Bombing, also go back to one day in September. My opinion every who wished to come into this country, are entitled to the American Dream. For those who desired a better future for their children's, by all means allowed into this country.

A Beatles song called "Revolution." The lyrics mention "if you talked about hate and destruction, brother you could counted me out." My message is the same thing with the Beatles lyrics.

Sincerely Johnny Wong

Beatles lyrics.

Sincerely

Dear Kristine :

Why did Japan lost the "Battle of Midway Islands?" Number one, America code breaker intercepted its messages. They're aware the Japanese invasions plans. My opinions their navel's code JN-25 was not very smart. JN could stood for Japanese Navy.

Vice Japanese admiral and their leaders was too over confidences, in wining this battle. Admiral Yamamoto plan was too complex. He set up a plan to invade the Aleutian Islands which belonged to Alaska. Hopping to draw the American fleet away from Midway.

He had four aircrafts carriers against three American carriers. Also an invasion forced consisted of light carriers and transports.

Luck was not on the Japanese side. Before the operations, two flying boats was going to refuel by submarines to spy on Pearl Harbor to see how many naval vessels, the United States had. Unfortunately, when they reached their destinations, the submarines' couldn't resurfaced to refuel the two flying boats, because the destroyers and cruisers' was anchored there.

Japan reconnaissance searched was poorly conducted, instead long range searched, they're only for a couple hundreds of miles. When the Americans flying boats sighted them, the elements of surprise was gone. Another crucial thing happened the cruiser, named "Tone", its message flying over the American vessels, "what might appeared ten vessels and a carrier." The message was delayed for half an hour, because something wrong with their radio. If the Japanese vice admiral received the communication earlier, the outcome of the battle might be chance.

Another mistake, his aircraft did not destroyed all of Midway Islands. His torpedoes' aircraft was armed with torpedoes, so he ordered them to switch to bombs go below deck. While this was happening Midway attacks, planes came and attack his carriers'.

When the message finally did arrived to him, ten vessels sighted, one what might be a carrier. The admiral was very unhappy, how could the American carrier's be out at sea? He had to make another crucial decisions. He felt the American carrier's was top priorities', Midway Islands could waited for a second attacks. The aircrafts that was armed with bombs had to go to the hanger deck, rearmed with torpedoes'. This will required about 60 minutes', times he might not have. While the crews was rearming, the torpedoes bombers from Enterprise, Hornet and Yorktown arrived, but without fighters coverage, they're sitting duck against the Japanese fighters named "Zero."

As the Japanese Zeros fighters shooting down the torpedoes bombers they're took them to sea level attitude, the Dauntless dive bombers from the two carriers came at the precise timing, they're unseen, in five minutes' crippled the Japanese carriers'.

Another luck was in the American was when the Japanese attack force chanced courses, Wade Causley of the Enterprise dived bombers decided to follow a destroyer, that was depth charging a U. S. Submarine, which let him to the Japanese Carriers forced.

My own opinion was that the Japanese vice admiral was wishing, washing, he took too much time from rearming torpedoes' to bombs and from bombs to torpedoes again. Those precious minutes caused him to loose the battle.

COMMENCEMENT ADDRESS PSCH

My first year in junior high school, as I viewed my text book, four picture of the globe. When Columbus discovered America, our world seems pretty round and big. When automobile was invented the Earth started to get a little smaller. As airline first appeared, time travel, a little quicker. Then with the intervention of computer, our universe once shrink in size.

Now a day with the arrival of computer, cell phone, internet services, email, electronic banking, ATM banking services, text sing, digital camera, camcorder, microwaves, videos movies, but nothing could take away things of the human heart, such as love, compassion, understanding, kindness, generosities, sweet, beauty, personalities from electronics and robotics' components.

Back during the 80's while I was in Boston, Toronto, New Jersey, and Hong Kong, receiving a letter or mailing a letter, making a long distance phone called meant much more, than all those things, I listed above. Being oversea in Canada, in Hong Kong, no greater joy when the operator answered the telephone and "said there's a Johnny Wong, calling from the British Crown Colony of Hong Kong, will you accepted the charge.?"

I didn't cared what illness or criminal convictions records, felonies, misdemeanors, some might be on probation, some even served jail time. I give everybody credits for getting out of bed, washed up, have breakfast, attending the program. At the same time I also understand people being fearful of mentally ill patients. Not a lot of people could worked with the psychical and mental, disable, got to show a lot of love, comforting, reaching out to them.

I am generous with people, I also at times, must cut back, to take care of my own needs, before I could reach out, comfort, meet the needs of others. I had to care of myself first.

Right now, I might run out of ideas, always liked to hear from what others opinions', could contributed to this world. Final message CONGRATION TO PSCH THE GLASS OF 2013 ! ! !

P.s. you have the key to unlock the future, this world is open, waiting for you.

Sincerely
Dear Kristine:

Kristine if you get a chance, looked under a famous military author by the name of Hector By Water. It was strange, to this day, I didn't knew if he was British or German by birth. Since he spoke two languages' fluently, he could passed by being an English or German spies.

His first novel entitled "Sea Power in the Pacific around 1936, mentioned the growing naval conflict between the United States and Japan. The government and the Japanese's militaries, always though the European and American government or military did not recognized Japan as an industrialized world power.

The Washington treaty and the London Naval treaty during the 1930's limited the size of Germany and Japan, plus all the nations of how many, what size of battleships or capital ships and the guns could be mounted on their forward and after turret.

Sea power in the Pacific predicted the growing tensions' between U.S. and Japan. With the invasion of Manchuria, the rape of Nanking when over 300,000 Chinese's, women, children's, yes including babies were mass murdered, the greatest Japanese armies violence, killings and the conquest of China during 1937 President Roosevelt put an oil embargo against the Japanese. He warned the military not to ship, irons, coals, strap metals, especially aviations' parts or gasoline's, without vital oils, the imperialist Japanese Navy, especially new battleships new aircraft carriers. Since she's an Island nations, her carriers forces basically depended the tankers to refuel them at sea.

Hector By Water knew it was only a matter of time before America and Japan was going to be at war with each other. Admiral Yamato was an Naval Attaché in Washington, even studied at Harvard University, even at one meeting got together, had a very pleasant, private convestions, with the a Japanese admiral.

One year before the attack on Pearl Harbor Hector By Water died of natural causes. Later on there's rumor he died of alcohol poisons'.

Johnny Wong

A GUITAR FINGERBOARD AND KEYBOARD, FOR A SPECIAL GIRL

Every boy good does another excellent.

Do Re Mi Fay So La Ti Do

A major C chord equal complement.

Mary had a little lamb.

A minor extremely another cute boy clam.

On a keyboard C, D, G equal Christ Dwell on Betty Glory.

Major D Chord attractive does her holy.

Bass clef middle C boldness, angel, greatness.

F notes, F sharp, G flat.

On a piano her playing format.

On a keyboard C Major, F Major G Major.

Your majesty court, folly gentle donor.

Beatles mania on your wedding.

"Across the universe."

It only takes a sparked, for a fuse.

"Can't buy me love."

Baking ham on a stove.

"A day in a life."

If you're cooking good as a chef.

"A goofy kind of love."

Getting a promotion considered approve.

Bryan Adams "we're in heaven."

While in the U.K. did you see Big Ben.

Christopher Cross, Air Supply, the Police speculate.

"Time after time", "Betty Davis eyes" Richard Marx "I'll be here waiting for you."

On a blind date, a cute Anglo guy considered a date.

Betty on your wedding date, read this poem to your handsome, cute future husband. By Johnny

PASSOVER FOR JULIE MAGARIL

What is Passover? It was in the book of Exodus, Ramses 11, an Egyptian Pharaoh battled with Moses concerning letting Israelis' go and worshiped their God's. God told the Jews "to sacrifice a lamb, painted a mark, in blood over the doorways." It represented the Jewish houses would be "Passover" First born of Egyptian would be sacrificed.

Julie her religion being Jewish. My religion a Christian. Sometime in common between us. She observed Passover, while I celebrated Good Friday and Easter. I don't cared what religion people were. Most vital thing if we're all lived in harmony, brotherly loved.

Each day we can't helped how we feel, when awaking up in the morning. They took survey, in the beginning most individuals liked their jobs, less than a year, considered to be very boring. I am not an law-enforcement, I don't carried a firearm. I am not police man of people actions.

Julie always believed in me, no matter how many years, she's had confident one day, I didn't have to take medications, have a job, lived normal lived.

As Christians believed in Good Friday. Where Christ suffering dieing on the cross, not easy for me to say this. I don't have the feeling, despised my mental conditions, I also asked God grace to forgive and lower my expectations on those who didn't meet my emotions needs.

Writing is never about getting fame, making a lot of monies. A good writer writes from his or her heart.

If I could writes to comfort, the good attributes' about Julie, I didn't needed to worry, pitying, feeling sorry for myself.

On this Passover, Good Friday and Easter, don't demanded, knew not easy, no matter what religions, let's showed a little love in our heart.